MW01426900

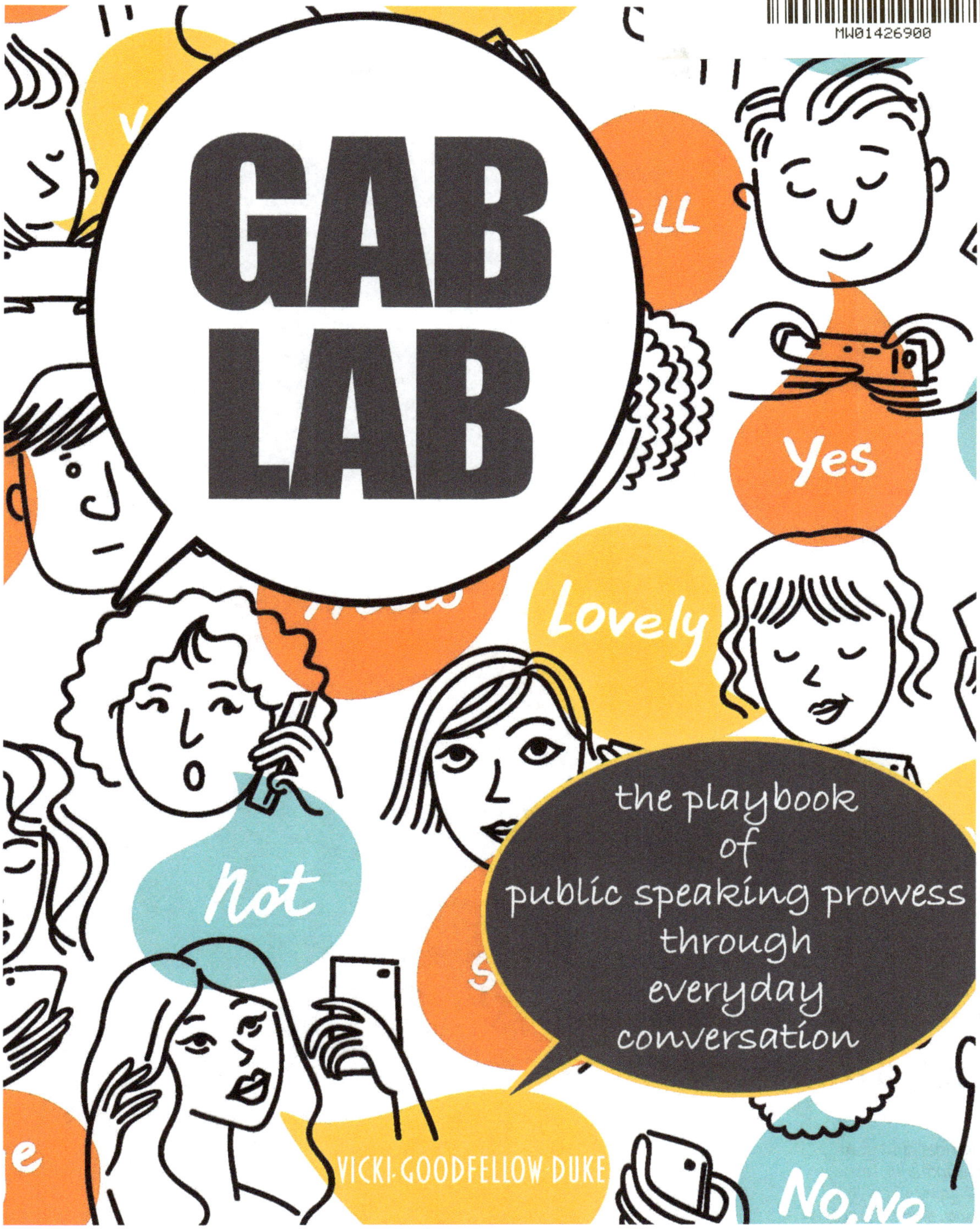
GAB LAB
the playbook of public speaking prowess through everyday conversation
VICKI GOODFELLOW DUKE
Yes
Lovely
Not

Kendall Hunt
publishing company

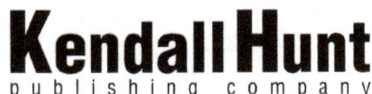

Cover © Shutterstock.com

www.kendallhunt.com
Send all inquiries to:
4050 Westmark Drive
Dubuque, IA 52004-1840

Copyright © 2020 by Kendall Hunt Publishing Company

ISBN: 978-1-7924-6038-8

All rights reserved. No part of this publication may be reproduced, stored in a retrieval system, or transmitted, in any form or by any means, electronic, mechanical, photocopying, recording, or otherwise, without the prior written permission of the copyright owner.

Published in the United States of America

Directory

Part I.
BIG IDEAS

- A. It's Just A Conversation 1
- B. Control Trumps Fear 11
- C. Impressions Matter 21
- D. Attention Needs Attention 31
- E. Data Overload Is Dangerous 37
- F. Beware Of The Competition 47
- G. Strategy Is Surefire 55

Part II.
PURPOSES

- A. CONNECT 63
- B. RESPOND 71
- C. INFORM 79
- D. NARRATE 99
- E. PERSUADE 111
- F. CELEBRATE 127
- G. ENTERTAIN 137

CITATIONS 145

It's Just A Conversation

You speak conversationally all the time.

Great public speaking is simply heightened conversation. This is worth repeating because it is so important: Great public speaking is heightened conversation.

© ISKRA_design/Shutterstock.com

Heightened: Prepared, designed, structured and rehearsed message

Conversation: Live, authentic and spontaneous in delivery, BASED ON and MADE POSSIBLE BY preparation.

PREPARATION: We give ample thought to our ideas; we plan; we design; we tweak; we create notes which allow us to speak conversationally; we practice and we practice and we practice.

DELIVERY: On the day, we show up and have an authentic conversation with our audience.

> The good news, in fact, the fantastic news, is that **anyone can become a great speaker by using strategies and practicing skills in their everyday conversations**. It is that simple.
>
> Many speakers wait for a live audience to hone their skills. This is a huge mistake. There are numerous chances every day to become a more organized, fluent and confident speaker if we take advantage of these opportunities in our everyday lives.

Conversational speaking uses the natural flow, form and vocabulary of everyday speech. The ear is attuned to processing and understanding spoken language. This oral style of communication varies significantly from the written style of communication. We can tell the difference, just by listening, between someone reading to us and someone speaking to us.

The differences are summarized in the chart below:

Written Style	Oral Style
Long, complex sentences	Simple, concise sentences
Many clauses per sentence	Few clauses per sentence
Formal or fancy vocabulary	Plain, everyday language
Carefully crafted and structured	Natural, relaxed
Pre-prepared, "dead"	Live, spontaneous
Tends to contain more abstractions	Tends to be more concrete

Why Does It Matter?

The Ear Does Not Effectively Process Written Language

The ear is not designed to process written language. It is designed to process spoken language. Written language is designed to be read. Think about reading a complex article which contains a number of new ideas and dense data. It is easy to miss important information even when we are able to control of the flow of the ideas by adjusting our own reading rate. If we are confused, we can easily go back and re-read the text. The same is not true for speaking. If the audience fails to process an idea, there is no replay button. Speakers have to ensure that their sentences are not overly long and complex.

Try reading this sentence, silently to yourself:

> *It is true that in the foreground, prior to fully comprehending the significance of loss, that we may fail to process the necessary steps which will allow us, once and for all, to stop undermining the processes which, for many of us, dictate our livelihoods.*

Now try having someone read it to you, aloud.

It is difficult to *hear* this sentence and to understand the point.

It should be noted that any writing that is designed to be read aloud, such as poetry, when done well, is designed with the ear in mind.

Long sentences have a hypnotic effect on the ear. Reading to people puts them to sleep. After all, there is a reason that we read bedtime stories to children.

If you want to put them to sleep, read the story. If you want to keep them awake, tell the story.

Conversational Style Allows for Flexibility

A prepared text locks the speaker into the message and allows no room for adaptation in the moment. Public speaking is not a monologue. It is a two-way process.

Speaker ⟶ Audience

Audience ⟶ Speaker

The messages go back and forth between the sender and receiver. It is easy to think of public speaking as a one-way street, but this is a mistake. Good speakers adjust and adapt according to the signals they receive from the audience. These signals are often, but not limited to, nonverbal signals. A good speaker will notice audience members frowning, in response to an explanation and will respond by explaining the concept in a different manner. A speaker may notice the audience becoming distracted and may respond by changing the data stream or using patterns interrupts. These techniques will be discussed in later chapters.

It may sound like an exaggeration to call prewritten text "dead" and spontaneous language "live" but there is a truth to this statement. There is a different energy to our speech when we find the right word at the right moment, when we look out into a room and respond with something that feels right at the time, based on our preparation.

Listeners Prefer Plain Language

Speak using plain, clear, concrete everyday language. Cheryl Stephens, author of *Plain Language in Plain English,* makes an excellent case for the necessity of using everyday language in our communications.

We like speakers better and report them as being more intelligent when they use everyday language. This is counterintuitive. We often assume that in order to sound and appear more intelligent that we should use fancy vocabulary in our presentations.

The problem is that speakers often muddle their own messages by trying to accomplish this very thing. We are not impressed by someone with a big vocabulary; we are impressed by someone who delivers a valuable, clear and memorable message.

It is a great idea to improve your own vocabulary by making new words a part of your vernacular, but replacing a clear simple word with another from a thesaurus dictionary may actually be a mistake, if it complicates the message.

Stephens is a proponent of the idea that we should aim for speaking to an audience at the level of a sixth grader. This technique is surprisingly effective in practice. It forces us to say exactly what we mean and nothing more. This is not equivalent to dumbing down the content of the message; it refers only to the way we explain concepts.

Delivery Affects Audience Memory and Recall

Memory encoding is a complex process. What concerns us here, is the process of *retrieving* memories. Once memories are stored, we need to be able to access them.

As explained by Daniel Levitin, author of *The Organized Mind*, associative access means that we can access our thoughts in a number of ways, through different associations, either semantic or perceptual, for example—a word, a picture, a song, a smell, etc. In order to recall a memory, we have to know where to look for it; if a memory is encoded in more than one form, it will be easier to recall because there are more associations with it.

For this reason, we may understand that images provide greater associative access than concepts. For example, if you need to remember *pomegranate*, you may retrieve and reconstruct the memory of that fruit by numerous associations including red, round, fruit, seeds, patterns, messy sour, etc. The image itself provides access. If you need to recall *solicitude*, what comes to mind? Likely not much, because this is a concept with very few if any associations, therefore little to no access is available. When memories are encoded as images, they can be retrieved more easily.

We are able to remember images with much greater recall than words (Grady et al. 1998; Paivio 1971; Shephard 1967).

For example, if you are asked to recall a memory from childhood, your brain searches its database to come up with a memory. That memory might look something like this:

> *I remember riding my little red tricycle down a hill in our backyard, when my uncle popped out of a bush, pushed me off my bike, hopped on and rode away while I rolled down the hill beside him.*

You recall that memory by accessing the image of the red bike, your uncle's laughing face, etc. You remember the images. You cannot remember the concept of being loved. You may infer the conclusion that you were loved, but you cannot remember it per se, as it is an abstract idea. Your audience's memory works in the same way.

Big Idea: It's Just A Conversation

Read the word list below. Then look away and see how many words you can recall.

- Sideways
- Annotate
- Regression
- Lip balm
- Lucid
- Driving range
- Refuse
- Yard
- Stoic
- Perpetuate
- Gloss
- Freedom
- Headboard
- Chicken
- Sophisticated

Lip balm, driving range, chicken, and maybe two more? These words are most likely to stick with you because they allow you to form mental images. When you can visualize a chicken, you recall the word. Abstract words are much harder to recall. Did anyone come up with an image for perpetuate?

Imagine that you watch a presentation. At the end of the presentation, the speaker says: As you leave here today, I would like you all to practice wellness.

As you walk out of the room, what do you do differently? Although you have a general understanding of the idea of practicing wellness, you cannot bring to mind a particular image.

Because there is no corresponding image, it is easily forgotten and not retrievable.

(Even if you do find an image that matches this idea, it may be completely different from someone else's image based on the same terminology. Practicing wellness to you might mean working out every day, while to your friend it might mean cutting calories and getting more sleep. Neither of you is correct or incorrect, because the idea is vague. It could be interpreted in any number of ways.)

The bottom line? *Speak to your audience so they can actively **visualize** your ideas*. This is especially important when it comes to asking them to take action at the end of a presentation.

Conversational Speaking Promotes Connection with Your Audience

The importance of forging a connection with your audience will be discussed in detail in the chapter entitled *Connect*, but suffice it to say here that connection is crucial. Conversational or extemporaneous speaking facilitates connection.

Modes of Speaking

Extemporaneous Mode

Ideally, great speakers use an extemporaneous mode of delivery. Extemporaneous speaking is conversational speaking using key word notes. These notes serve as triggers or reminders for us to elaborate on a particular idea. They are not word for word notes. Extemporaneous speeches, even when rehearsed a number of times, will never be the same twice. A slight change in wording, an additional example, a change in rate, tone, and delivery . . . there are many ways in which the speech may change when a speaker speaks with key word notes, but the core ideas will remain unchanged.

In order for this kind of speaking to work, the speaker's notes must facilitate, not prevent, conversational delivery. Steps to prepare key word notes appear in the chapters entitled *Respond* and *Inform*.

There are three additional modes of delivery. Each of these modes will be used effectively in a particular context and each has serious downfalls when used outside such contexts.

Manuscript Mode

Manuscript mode requires a speaker to read a prewritten, word for word text to the audience.

As mentioned earlier, reading aloud to the audience is not the most effective way to communicate, as it attempts to mix the oral and written styles of communication.

While a written manuscript contains the inherent problems mentioned earlier (long, complex sentences and formal vocabulary) there is an additional downfall to this mode which involves the speaker's delivery. This problem will be discussed at greater length in the chapter entitled *Connect,* but for now, remember that it is very difficult to hold an audience's attention when you are relying on a word for word script. Your eyes are glued to the page!

Can manuscript mode ever be effective?

Manuscript mode can be effective and sometimes, but rarely, necessary. A speaker who is highly accountable for each word he utters, perhaps delivering precise and important data, may choose to use manuscript delivery. (Think: politician delivering a budget, or legislator delivering legislation.)

Professional speechwriters often write manuscript speeches to be read by a speaker, giving the impression that the speaker is speaking conversationally. Good speechwriters are masters at this technique; it is not easy for the average speaker to accomplish the task successfully.

If you need to deliver a manuscript presentation, and the benefits outweigh the costs, keep the following in mind:

1. Say aloud, what you intend to communicate. Then, write it down. NOT the other way around.
2. Tweak the language and sentence structure so that it mimics spoken language. Avoid overly long sentences and avoid too many abstract nouns.
3. Rehearse the manuscript over and over again.
4. Place the text to the side, away from the body. Use your thumb to slide down the page, thereby marking your spot in the text, allowing you to look up and make eye contact with your audience as you read.
5. Pay attention to your delivery, making sure that you sound conversational and not robotic.

It is very reasonable to read a small portion of text during a presentation, in manuscript style, if necessary.

Memorized Mode

Memorized mode is based on a prewritten manuscript. Therefore, with the exception of reading aloud, all of the problems that pertain to manuscript delivery also pertain to memorized delivery.

Memorized delivery poses an additional challenge: memorization. It takes time to memorize a word for word script. The challenge in delivery is the recall of exact wording which puts significant stress on the speaker. If a speaker forgets the wording during delivery, he is forced to resort to conversational speaking which will lead to a lack of congruence in speaking style. This lack of congruence is noticeable to the audience and may result in a loss of speaker credibility.

A memorized delivery poses the risk of appearing like a performance rather than a presentation. Public speakers do not perform, they present. The difference lies in the authentic nature of self-expression. Speakers do not become characters or take on other roles, but attempt to represent themselves and their ideas authentically, honestly and directly.

There are occasions where a speaker may wish to memorize a small piece of text such as a quote, or a poem etc., for dramatic effect but the presentation in its entirety should not be memorized.

Impromptu Mode

Impromptu speaking is defined as speaking with no prior preparation. By definition then, conversation itself is impromptu speaking. We rarely, if ever, preplan our conversations and seem to manage to communicate effectively, for the most part. This should be a point of encouragement. Those who converse on a regular basis already possess a degree of proficiency which transfers to a public speaking setting.

Preparation is obviously preferable to a lack of preparation. We should never choose to speak impromptu when we have the opportunity to be prepared in advance. Preparation allows us to be certain of our ideas, to structure them and to rehearse the message.

© studiostoks/Shutterstock.com

Conversation

Every conversation requires active listening by all participants. From a speaking perspective, conversation takes a three-part form: ask, comment, and share. While this form tends to occur naturally in an easy conversation, the structure provides a strategy for a speaker who has difficulty keeping a conversation flowing. Not everybody is a great conversationalist, so this can be helpful if you are stuck sitting beside a stranger at a wedding, or chatting with a shy colleague. It can help stimulate a natural flow of ideas when we don't know someone well and are unsure of appropriate topics.

It's very simple, and we use it already.

Now remember it with intention:

Ask: Ask a question

Questions beginning with *what* or *how* are usually a safe bet. It may be wise to avoid questions beginning with *why* until a trust relationship is formed, as *why* questions may unintentionally sound challenging or confrontational.

What do you think of this?

What would you do differently next time?

How do you feel about this?

How did this happen?

Etc.

Active Listening: If you have actively listened to the speaker's response, it will be easy to offer an appropriate comment.

Big Idea: It's Just A Conversation

Comment: Make an appropriate reply

That's interesting.

I didn't know that.

Tell me more about this aspect.

I'd like to more about your experience.

Etc.

Share: Offer information

Sharing information or a personal experience, based on the topic at hand is an excellent way to keep a conversation going. You will see in the chapter entitled *Connect*, that there is an important reason for you to share information as well as ask and comment.

I had a similar experience once....

That reminds me of something that happened to me....

Our business focuses on......

Etc.

The three forms can be used in any combination:

Ask, comment, share,

Ask, share

Share, ask

Share, comment,

Comment, comment, comment, etc.

It's not rocket science, but it helps to have a plan.

> **EVERYDAY CONVERSATION PRACTICE:**
>
> Strengthen conversation skills by having a specific strategy for when conversation becomes difficult or awkward. Having a strategy allows the speaker to have a plan rather than struggling to say something.
>
> And sure. You can try it over the phone.
>
> 1. **Ask. Share. Comment.** Try this strategy when you meet someone new or are having an "awkward" conversation.
> 2. **Use Concrete Language.** Try this in conversation. It will make your communication clearer and more memorable, while building good speaking habits.

Control Trumps Fear

Fear is not the enemy.

Fear is the SPARK

that ignites change.

Fear of public speaking is very common. Some studies have ranked the fear of public speaking higher than the fear of death. While it is easy to label ourselves as nervous speakers and leave it at that, fortunately, fear of public speaking can be overcome.

Making two simple changes is the secret to overcoming fear of public speaking:

Change in Mindset

Change in Habits

© Valeriya_Dor/Shutterstock.com

Change in Mindset

The way we think informs both our future thoughts and our behaviors.

Fear is a *mental habit*.

The first small change in mindset is an important one.

Often, we see ourselves as nervous speakers who desire to become confident. It is easy, therefore to see only the extreme ends of the spectrum. There is, however, a full spectrum between the two extremes.

© best4u/Shutterstock.com   © best4u/Shutterstock.com   © best4u/Shutterstock.com

Becoming a confident speaker is a *process.* Instead of thinking of yourself as an anxious speaker (the face on the left) think of yourself as being in the process of becoming a confident speaker (somewhere in the middle of the spectrum). This small mindset shift will influence your view of yourself, because we live up to the labels we give ourselves (both positive and negative). This small shift will allow you to move forward.

Fear of a Lack of Control

Some **studies** suggest that what we fear, in all circumstances, is the fear of a lack of control. For example, if you fear losing your job, your fear is really a fear of not knowing how you would survive a job loss, or fear of the lack of control. If you fear that a family member may become ill, what you really fear is how you would handle such a misfortune.

According to Susan Jeffers (2019), author of *Feel the Fear and Do It Anyway,* we fear the inability to

© studiostoks/Shutterstock.com

"handle" something. Understandably, we don't like the feeling of loss of control. Pushing through the fear is actually less frightening than dealing with the fear that stems from the feeling of helplessness.

When it comes to the fear of public speaking, it is important to realize that the more control we have, the less that fear will bother us. There are a number of areas where we can increase our sense of control. We also must acknowledge when and where we do not have control and to stop worrying about what we have no power to control.

What We Cannot Control

Others' thoughts
Others' perceptions of us
Others' opinions
Others' behavior
Our thoughts at point A*

What We Can Control

Our own thoughts
Our own words
Our own behavior
Our preparation
Our thoughts at point B*

We are much stronger and more versatile than we usually acknowledge; we need to trust in our abilities to handle difficulties and challenges.

The biggest concern with control lies in fear physiology.

Fear Physiology

You are more than likely familiar with the Fight, Flight, or Freeze response. (FFF)

Here are a few important points about FFF.

1. It is an involuntary state. We don't choose to enter into the state and therefore we cannot choose to exit the state. Due to this lack of control, we want to avoid getting into the state in the first place.

2. Your body responds similarly to all fear experiences, both life-threatening (being chased by a bear) and non-life-threatening (being afraid to give a speech). Increased adrenaline, racing heart, and shallow breath may help you when you're fighting off a bear, but will be a detriment when you have to stand in front of an audience.

3. FFF triggers a neurochemical response in the brain with the production of stress hormones: norepinephrine and cortisol, etc. These hormones put the neural pathways on lockdown in order to protect brain tissue and conserve resources.

4. For a speaker, who is trying to think and speak at the same time, the prefrontal cortex needs to send messages via neural pathways to other parts of the brain. These neurochemicals prevent that communication from happening. When the brain is on lockdown, we find it difficult to transfer ideas to speech. We blank out easily or forget what we have said, after the fact.

5. In order for FFF to activate, a trigger must be present. The trigger for speakers, unfortunately, comes from our internal thoughts.

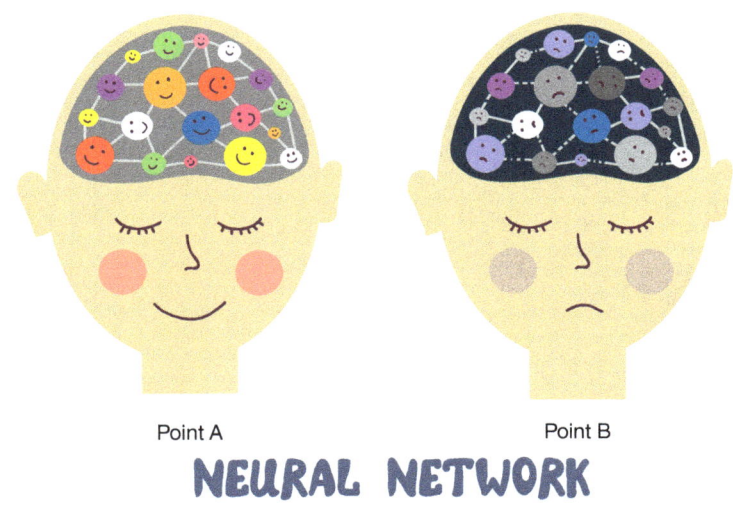

© Tetyana Snezhyk/Shutterstock.com

Again, we will discuss control: what we can and cannot control as it pertains to thoughts.

Point A: A thought comes to you.

(No control)

We cannot control the thoughts that enter our minds.

Point B: Once the thought has "landed" we have two choices.

(Both choices are within our control.)

1. To engage with the thought/mentally elaborate.

2. To dismiss the thought.

Let's break down these two options at Point B.

1. **Elaborate**: When we elaborate on a thought (positive or negative) we grow neural pathways. The more similar thoughts we have, the more those pathways grow. For example, when you were in high school you factored polynomials. You probably got quite good at it and were able to do equations quickly. What about now? Do you

remember how to factor a polynomial? Most adults do not. Why? Because they haven't used those pathways in a long time and the pathways have shrunk due to lack of use. If we stop elaborating on negative thoughts about public speaking, our habitual pathways will shrink from lack of use and disappear from long-term memory. It is crucial, however, to deal with short-term memory first.

2. **Dismiss**: Dismissing thoughts can be challenging because thoughts seem to persist especially when we don't want them. It is possible to develop mental discipline, so we know exactly what to do with unwanted thoughts. Negative thoughts must be eliminated because of the damage they do, both in the short-term (put us into FFF mode) and in the long-term (multiply negative neural pathways). In order to dismiss negative thoughts, we implement the Fly Technique.

Fly Technique

When a negative thought "lands" immediately dismiss the thought by flicking it away, in the same way you would flick away a fly that has landed on your arm. Don't give the thought any attention. Just flick.

The first fifty times you try this exercise, you may think it won't work, because the thoughts keep returning. Be persistent. The thoughts keep returning because they are habits. This process will break the habit and shrink the pathways.

Immediately after flicking the thought away, distract yourself with something that forces you to concentrate or "think hard". (Try adding large numbers in your head or recall world capitals, etc.) It is important that we activate System 2 Thinking (more on that in another chapter). System 2 requires deep concentration. We want to deactivate the fear response of the amygdala and activate the analytical mode.

© kusumai/Shutterstock.com

To recap:

Flick and Distract.

Note: Do NOT try to replace a negative thought with its opposite positive thought unless you believe the positive thought to be true. We know when we are lying to ourselves and we don't like it.

If the thought comes to you: *I hate public speaking*—don't try to replace it with *I love public speaking.* It won't work and you will feel like a fake.

The more often you practice this technique, the more quickly the negative thoughts will dissipate and fail to bother you.

Changing Our Habits

© Limolida Design Studio/Shutterstock.com

Developing new strategies and speaking habits are the secret to becoming a stronger and more confident speaker.

The strategies will be outlined in Part II. The quickest and most effective way to change habits is by replacing old habits with new ones. Daily practice is the best and easiest way to accomplish this task. We don't need an audience to practice public speaking. Small changes make a big impact.

Breathe Like a (Navy) Seal

Navy Seals are known for their ability to take important action in highly stressful, often unpredictable situations.

A former U.S. Navy Seals Commander explains how to use box breathing to combat the shallow uncontrolled breathing that we tend to practice in stressful situations.

Forbes: How to De-Stress in 5 Minutes or Less According to a Navy Seal

https://www.forbes.com/sites/nomanazish/2019/05/30/how-to-de-stress-in-5-minutes-or-less-according-to-a-navy-seal/#7229ded13046

Anchoring

Sometimes we can overanalyze the cause of our fears and anxieties. While they are interesting to study on a psychological level, it is not necessary to find the root of fears in order to overcome them. Theory is not necessary for change; enforcing new habits is the key.

What we know about learning is that we do not learn when we are completely comfortable, nor do we learn when we are very uncomfortable. In these cases we are either too complacent for growth, or too busy trying to survive. There is a sweet spot (X) between comfort and discomfort. This is where growth takes place.

COMFORT   X   DISCOMFORT

Allowing yourself to move out of your comfort zone will help you to grow quickly. Taking small steps is the most effective way to do this.

A very effective way to change your comfort level is by a process called Anchoring, taken from NLP, or Neuro-Linguistic Programming (Campbell 2018; Zaharia, Reiner, and Schutz 2015).

An anchor is a point which is still in your comfort zone but that is closest to your goal.

1. Identify your anchor
2. Start speaking in your anchor and take a small step into discomfort zone
3. With practice, what was once the discomfort zone will become new anchor

Identify Your Anchor

Imagine that you are afraid of snakes. Your *goal* (which we will also call the *100%*) is to be comfortable with a snake wrapped around your neck. Maybe you want a great photo (shrug). At the moment, having a snake around your neck is going to send you into panic mode. It is not the right place to start.

Ask yourself: how close can I get to the snake *while remaining in my comfort zone?* What about if I hold the snake beside you? (Still too close)

What about if the snake is across the room? (Don't like that either)

What about if the snake is behind glass? (Ok. That will work)

Being near a snake which is behind glass is as close as you can get, right now, to your goal, while still being comfortable. This is called your anchor.

Once you have found your anchor, you are going to transition a single experience from your anchor to a first small step into discomfort.

Example:

You look at the snake behind glass (anchor) but as you are looking at it, partway through, someone brings the snake out from behind the glass into the same room.

This is a biohack to trick your brain into reacting the same way to discomfort as it does to comfort.

Fortunately, this is easier in public speaking than it is with snakes!

Let's say your goal is to be comfortable standing and speaking in front of a live audience of 500 people. If we put you there now, you will experience severe discomfort and won't learn anything. Ask yourself: *how close can I get to this goal while still in my comfort zone?*

Take time to find the answer.

Am I comfortable.....

Standing, speaking in front of 100 people? (Definitely not)

Standing, speaking in front of 50 people? (No)

Standing, speaking in front of 25 people? (Not much better)

Standing, speaking in front of 10 people? (No)

Standing, speaking in front of 5 people? (Better, but not great)

Sitting, speaking in front of 5 people? (Almost!)

Sitting, speaking in front of 2 people? (Yes. I can do that.)

Let's say that sitting down, speaking in front of two people is your anchor. **This is where all of your practice sessions should begin.**

You may not have a live audience for practice, but finding a picture of two people, putting it on your laptop screen and sitting in front of the picture will do the trick. Your brain will do the rest.

Start speaking in your anchor. Then, midway through a sentence, stand up and keep speaking. Don't make a big deal in your mind about the position change. You are re-training your brain to treat this new position in the same way it treats the anchor.

Once you repeat this a couple of times, your brain will see them as being the same. The new position will become your new anchor.

Gradually, you can keep changing your anchor until you are comfortable with a photo of an audience of 500 people. When you experience a live audience of the same size, it will no longer be a big deal. Your brain will have become accustomed and will no longer activate your fear response.

Steepling

Steepling is a hand position that can help a speaker feel more confident. There are nerve endings at the tips of the fingers; when the finger-tips come together, a message is delivered to the brain. This is based

Biohack
© jesadaphorn/Shutterstock.com

on the fact that the brain delivers messages to the body, but that the body also delivers messages to the brain. It is the latter process that enables steepling to work effectively.

In the same way that we naturally cross arms in front of us when stressed or defensive, when we are feeling confident and relaxed, we naturally use hand steepling. The nerve impulses which deliver the message to the brain communicate that we are feeling confident and relaxed, even if we are not actually feeling that way. The position itself is a biohack.

If the steepling position is held for at least thirty seconds, the brain is tricked into thinking that confidence is our present state and the body proceeds to produce more "happy" neurochemicals such as endorphins and dopamine. The production of these chemicals will then cause us to *legitimately* experience the relaxed confident state. Think of this state as being the opposite state to the FFF. When the body is relaxed, the mind fully alert and so focused on the task at hand that we lose track of time and place, we call this the **flow state** (Csikszentmihaly 2009).

Vulnerablity: The Good News

As speakers, worry about being imperfect increases our fear. We imagine all the worst-case scenarios: What if my technology doesn't work? What if I make a mistake? What if I forget what I was going to say? What if the audience doesn't agree with my position on the topic?

There has been a good deal of research on the psychology of vulnerability. Brene Brown, while not the only one collecting data, is the face of the research.

The Power of Vulnerability Brene Brown

https://youtu.be/X4Qm9cGRub0

© 360b/Shutterstock.com

In a nutshell:

While many of us spend time and energy attempting to appear perfect to others, the research shows that people like us better and are able to connect with us more easily when they see us as imperfect.

This is great news for public speakers!

Not only will our imperfections fail to ruin our chance of being likeable, they will actually increase our likeability. So, while no one wants to fall on their face while approaching the stage, or drop their notecards, these things can work for us, if they do happen. It all depends on how we handle the situation.

Have a sense of humor.

Remember that you are not perfect. Neither is anyone in your audience. We are all human. Don't overfuss a mistake. Laugh. Relax. Acknowledge the mistake if the audience has already noticed it. If they haven't noticed, then carry on; it is your secret.

Fear of Judgment

Fear of judgment is perhaps the most common source of fear among speakers.

Initially, when we think of judgment, we need to recall what we can and cannot control. There is little value in obsessing about what we do not have the power to change.

Your job as a speaker is to be authentic and to be as prepared as possible.

There is no guarantee that everyone in the room will agree with your ideas, but this is no different than our experience in the external world.

In our everyday lives we encounter many individuals from different backgrounds, with varied tastes, attitudes and values. We know that we are different and we accept those differences. While we prefer that others agree with our views, we acknowledge that we live in a diverse world. We know that we can't please everyone. We don't give too much attention to seeking validation from everyone we encounter in our daily lives, so why do we seek that validation in a room full of people? What is the difference? The answer is that there is no difference. The difference lies only in our perceptions.

Remember that your audience is a microcosm of the world. Be yourself. Be authentic. You are enough. You are unique. Be prepared. Do your best.

> **Everyday Conversation Practice:**
>
> **1. Try the anchoring exercise** above using the practice audiences in the deck below.
> **A Practice Audience Deck**
> https://www.haikudeck.com/p/d72f5fd860
>
> **2. Practice flicking away negative thoughts pertaining to public speaking.** It can be tedious work, but you will achieve results with perseverance.
>
> **3.** To accelerate the eradication of negative thoughts, **try flicking away ALL negative thoughts**. You will re-wire your brain to attract positive rather than negative thoughts. You will form new, healthy mental habits.

Impressions Matter

© GLYPHstock/Shutterstock.com

How long do you have to make a first impression?

Ten minutes

Five minutes

Two minutes

Thirty seconds

Fifteen seconds

Seven seconds

Two seconds

You have seven seconds to convince your audience that you are worthy of their attention.

The countdown begins as soon as the audience can see you.

Reasonable? No
Rational? No
Realistic? Yes

It is important to mention that first impressions are not everything; they can be changed. However, due to our tendency as humans to fall victim to confirmation bias, where we like to be consistent with our first impressions, it is difficult to change someone's mind once they have made a decision.

Harvard Business professor and social psychologist Amy Cuddy has been studying first impressions for over fifteen years. Her findings show that in the first seven seconds, the audience is subconsciously looking for you to demonstrate two qualities: competence and warmth.

Competence and Warmth

Competence

In order to pay attention, we need to believe that a speaker has something to offer beyond what we already know, that they are an expert in the field, that they have both knowledge and experience.

We actually form impressions before significant content can be shared; after all, how much can someone say in just seven seconds?

It is evident, then, that impressions of competence are not based on content. What are they based upon if not upon content? Since we have only limited information available to us, we form impressions based on a speaker's non-verbals.

Nonverbals

Nonverbals include appearance, dress, and body language. While the first two considerations are relevant, they are much less responsible for the conclusions reached by the audience. A high percentage of nonverbal messaging stems from body language: stance, gesture, movement, and facial expression.

Stance

The way you stand determines how you will be perceived. Stance can broadcast confidence or nervousness. Remember that it doesn't really matter if the conclusions are accurate or not; people will form an impression based on how they perceive you.

Position	Impression
Feet together	Passive, submissive, proper
Feet crossed	Universal sign for *I have to pee*
One foot in front	Awkward
Feet turned out	Misplaced ballerina
Feet shoulder-width apart	Confidence, authority

Movement—Should I Move?

With regard to movement, we always want to avoid two extremes: moving constantly (the pacing professor) and not moving at all (the robot).

Move when there is a purpose to do so. Movement should complement your ideas. When your ideas shift in topic or tone, your body should shift too. This movement will visually emphasize the change in ideas.

If you have a large space, it is a good idea to use the space by taking a few steps to the right or left, in accordance with the principle laid out above.

If you are speaking in a tight space, you can achieve the same result by simply shifting your weight from one foot to another in between your points and then immediately return to placing the weight evenly on the balls of both feet. This minor shift movement has the same transitional effect.

You can plan to move at important transition points in the presentation, but remember to keep still while delivering an important idea. Movement will distract and lessen the impact of a strong idea.

The more comfortable you become as a speaker, the more natural and intuitive your movement will become.

Hands

The placement of hands and arms is extremely important. This placement alone can make or break your credibility.

If asked your opinion on speaking with arms crossed in front of the chest, most people would say that this position is not effective. You may have been told this information, but more likely than not, you know it intuitively. We associate arms crossed in front of the chest as being defensive or closed. The reason we easily make this association is that when we naturally feel defensive or angry, we adopt this position. It happens involuntarily, with the help of the limbic system. Since the limbic system is tied to emotional state and acts in real time, we don't always know what our bodies are doing. If we are nervous, there are particular physical tells which manifest in the body.

Hand Position	Impression
Arms crossed in front of chest	Defensive, angry, closed
Hands behind back	Untrustworthy
Hands in pockets	Untrustworthy
Hands clasped in front of body	Nervous, closed
Arms crossed at wrists	Nervous, closed
Hands on hips	Aggressive
Arms hanging by side	Low energy, disinterested
Steepling	High confidence, authority
Hands at waist level, away from body	High confidence, authority

Apparently, we don't trust someone if we cannot see their hands. For this reason, hands behind back and in pockets are not a good idea.

Hands in front of the body give the same negative impression as arms crossed because they block the chest and audience from the audience's view. In fact, hands or arms in front of the body are the "lite" version of arms crossed.

While this will be discussed in a later chapter, it is important to mention here that *anything* that is placed between the speaker's chest/abdomen and the audience is considered a *block* and should be avoided. This includes: podium (yes, really) desk, paper, notecards, etc.

The only two positions which deliver a positive impression are steepling and hands away from the body at waist level. This latter position is called the Circle of Power. (COP) In the COP, your hands never go above your eyes, or below your waist; they remain in this imaginary circle.

Neither position should come across as a pose. We want to look and feel natural while giving a positive impression. The more you practice these positions in everyday conversations, the more natural the positions will feel and the more habitual they will become.

Gestures—Should I Use Them?

Yes, and no.

Gestures, or hand movements, come naturally to some people when they speak. If you talk with your hands, then yes, go ahead and do so. Talking with the hands can be such a habit that many people don't even know the extent to which they do it; for that reason, don't try to keep hands still, because due to habit, they will be flapping at your sides anyway, looking like flippers.

Never, ever, plan a gesture, unless you are also a professional actor. If you have to practice a cheer in front of the mirror, which you intend to pull out at the six-minute mark of your speech, complete with a "Yahoo" it's going to come across as a performance. A presentation is never a performance. We associate performances with acting but we expect authenticity from a presenter. In this case, no, do not plan and use a gesture. It is too easy to lose credibility if you look like you are performing.

If however, in the moment you feel a spontaneous urge to cheer and shout "Yahoo"— then do it, because in that live moment, that gesture will come from a place of truth. We will like it because we will believe it.

Warmth

In addition to appearing competent, we must also demonstrate warmth. Warmth may be defined as friendliness, likeability and trustworthiness.

These qualities can be demonstrated in various ways throughout a conversation or presentation, but the initial impressions of warmth come from a genuine smile and from eye contact.

© sangdaeng/Shutterstock.com

Smile

A genuine smile is easily detectable from a fake smile. A genuine smile, also called the Duchenne smile, activates the zygomaticus major muscle and the orbicularis oculi muscle while a fake smile primarily engages the mouth and cheek muscles.

The problem is that if we are nervous, it can be tricky to break into a genuine smile in those first seven seconds. Believe it or not, this is also something that can be improved upon with practice.

A real smile comes from a positive emotion, which stems from either a thought or from something in our environment. Since we can't rely on an unpredictable environment, the trigger for a real smile must come from our thoughts. The gracious host technique is useful to practice until it becomes second nature.

Gracious Host Technique

Imagine that you are having friends over for dinner. You spend the whole day cleaning, if you're like most people and cooking. Sometimes we are running around the house at the last minute doing little jobs that need to be done. However, when the doorbell rings, we know that we have to stop working and attend to our guests. Even if you didn't clean the downstairs bathroom to your liking, you know it's too late now.

When you open the door to your guests, you spend every ounce of energy on them, making them feel welcome and comfortable in your home, after all, you are the host.

By imagining the audience as "guests" rather than a collection of strangers, our limbic system is activated to respond with positive signals. Treating the audience like guests helps the speaker to focus on the audience, rather than on himself. This can help alleviate nerves.

Because we generally like people whom we invite to our home, there is a natural kind of intimacy that occurs when we speak to our friends. We smile real smiles; our vocal tone is warm and expressive; our body language is open and relaxed. We are not putting on an act; we are authentically demonstrating warmth.

Eye Contact

Eye contact is challenging for many speakers. We know that we need to look at the audience, but somehow that task seems daunting and we would rather avoid the discomfort of making eye contact with strangers.

Again, if we re-imagine the audience as guests, the task becomes easier.

Let's discuss what not to do, before we discuss what is effective. This is important because there are many myths in existence which suggest that we can avoid true eye contact when speaking to an audience. These myths have been suggested and popularized by familiar speaking sources. Perhaps they seemed legitimate at the time, but we now know better.

Myth A:

Don't worry about looking at the audience. Just look at the back wall.
We can tell that you're not looking at us. We wonder what's back there!

Myth B:

You don't need to look at people's eyes, just look at the top of their heads.
Wrong. We can tell the difference.

Myth C:

Just look straight ahead.
Wrong. There is more than one person in your audience.

Myth D:

Keep your head still and move your eyes.
Honestly, this will make people laugh out loud. If your goal is to look like an escaped criminal, go for it. Otherwise, avoid at all costs.

Myth E:

Move your head constantly back and forth, left to right, right to left.
This action makes your head seem like it's on a mechanical arm. Not a great look.
Avoid, unless you want the nickname swivelhead.

The best way to make authentic eye contact is to use the technique called One Thought, One Person.

One Thought, One Person Technique

Your audience is made up of individual human beings, each one different and unique. Therefore, treat your audience as a group of individual people and speak to them one person at a time. This mimics conversational speaking!

Lock eye contact with a single person, and deliver to them a complete idea—usually one or two sentences (McAfee and Wallace 2019). When you are looking at this person, you can forget that there is anyone else in the room. Use all of your energy to make sure *this one person* has a good experience, that *this one person* understands your ideas, that *this one person* has your full attention.

Once you have delivered this one thought, move your eyes across the room to another single individual. Speak to them with the same concern, energy and focus as you deliver a single thought.

Be sure to include listeners in all areas of the room, one at a time. Everyone will feel included because of the short length of time that you spend with each person and because you include people in all areas of the room.

From the audience's perspective, this is great, because you are actually talking *to* them, not at them. It feels like an intimate conversation.

From a speaker's perspective, there is also a big advantage. You feel much more relaxed because it really doesn't matter how many people are in the room, when you approach them one at a time.

Delivery Skills: Energy, Volume, Articulation, Rate, Pause, Emphasis

Delivery skills matter to the degree that they allow the speaker to be effective.

Oftentimes a speaker's delivery presents barriers for the audience.

Energy

Public speaking delivery requires immense energy. It's like having a conversation with 600 times the horsepower.

You should use low, diaphragmatic breathing to energize the cells and muscles in your body as well as supporting your voice.

Tonicity means that the body utilizes a degree of energy that you would use to play a sport. Sustained physical energy is draining, which is why, after a presentation done well, you may feel physically exhausted.

Speak Up: Vocal Energy

If your listeners can't hear you very well, because you are not projecting your voice in a large space, you will lose their attention very quickly. Listeners are generally lazy. Unless the audience is motivated to sit on the edge of their chairs and lean forward to hear you because they are dying to hear your content, they will instead tune out and disengage.

Articulate

Articulate your words carefully. Don't mumble.

Watch especially at the ends of sentences; without adequate breath support and vocal energy, the words or sounds at the ends of sentences may be swallowed. In the English language, often the most important word comes at the end of the sentence.

© studiostoks/Shutterstock.com

For example:

The one thing I would change about myself, if I could, is my blabla.

This project is very important and we need to immediately implement blabla.

The secret to leading a successful life is blabla

In each case, if you miss the last word in the sentence, you have missed the whole point.

Rate

Slow your regular speaking rate when you are speaking in front of an audience. A rushed speaker is not a good speaker. Racing through ideas will not only make you stressed and exhausted, but it gives a negative impression to your audience. Rushed speakers appear nervous and less credible than their more controlled counterparts.

Remember that although these ideas are very familiar to you, they are new to the audience. Listeners need time to process new information in order to understand and retain it. (More on this in *Data Overload Is Dangerous*) Audiences find it harder to listen to fast-talkers because of the energy it requires just to keep up with them.

Be especially careful with rate of delivery on numerical data, or complex ideas. Take. Your. Time.

Changing the speaking rate throughout the presentation will ensure that you hold your audience's attention. Avoid falling into a predictable monotone, mono-rate delivery.

Pause

Pauses allow the speaker to breathe and re-group, while they allow the audience the necessary time to form mental schemas—categorizing and storing the new information.

Pauses may also be used for effect.

Emphasis

All ideas are not equal. Decide which ideas are most important and be deliberate in making these ideas come to the forefront.

One way to emphasize ideas is to use the following technique from *Voice and Diction* by Lyle Mayer:

Emphasis Technique:

1. Speak at your regular rate.
2. Just before an important idea, use a pause. (When you stop talking people will look up to see if you are still alive.)
3. Now that you have everyone's full attention, change your rate. Speak more quickly, or slow down. Generally more important ideas demand a slow rate.
4. Pause again. This pause gives the audience time to process the new idea.
5. Resume original speaking rate.

We can also emphasize ideas by changing **volume**, and **pitch**.

It has been suggested that listeners recall anywhere from 7 to 30 percent of your content. (Let's just say 30 percent would be hitting the jackpot)

Choose what you want the audience to remember. Then emphasize it in your delivery.

EVERYDAY CONVERSATION PRACTICE

1. **Practice the correct stance for speaking.** Use it any time you are standing and having a conversation. The goal is to make it a habit. Remember that first impressions are important in interpersonal conversations such as networking, as well as in public speaking.

2. **Practice using steepling and the Circle of Power** when having everyday conversations. Again, the goal is forming new habits.

3. Be intentional about incorporating **warmth** into your interpersonal interactions, especially when meeting someone for the first time.

4. **Practice using one thought, one person when speaking to two or more individuals.** You can try this in a meeting, on video chats or at the kitchen table.

Attention Needs Attention

© studiostoks/Shutterstock.com

Goals: Attention, Comprehension, Retention

In any presentation, a speaker should have three goals: Attention, Comprehension and Retention. Regardless of the specific purpose of a presentation, these three goals are crucial because without any one of them effective communication is not possible.

The first order of business in delivering any presentation is gaining attention—the kind of attention where the audience is really listening, focusing intently on your message, engaging with you and your ideas. It is only then that comprehension and retention are possible.

This kind of attention cannot exist when people are staring at their laptops or phones, or fading in and out of attention from internal distractions.

While we cannot completely prevent listeners from daydreaming or being distracted due to the nature of the human condition, we can dramatically reduce the likelihood of these occurrences by making conscious, deliberate choices.

Initial Setup

The beginning of a meeting or presentation is the optimal time to set out your expectations as a speaker. While it is not possible 100 percent of the time, it is often within your control to simply request that your audience put away laptops or phones before you begin to speak. Ask politely and firmly. Most people will comply with this request without giving it a second thought. People open laptops in meetings because it is a habit for them to do so. If they are worried about taking notes, it is easy enough to provide pen and paper or to ensure that you will provide takeaway notes or slides following the presentation. Don't be afraid to ask. It is your time to speak.

Gaining Attention

If we don't have the audience's attention at the very beginning of a presentation, it is very difficult to get their attention at all.

Numerous studies including (Arnsten and Li 2004; Hollerman and Schultz 1998; Stauffer and Lak 2017) have examined the physiology of paying attention, looking at what happens in the human body when a person is fully engaged in a state of heightened attention. The results of these studies enable us to reverse engineer audience attention.

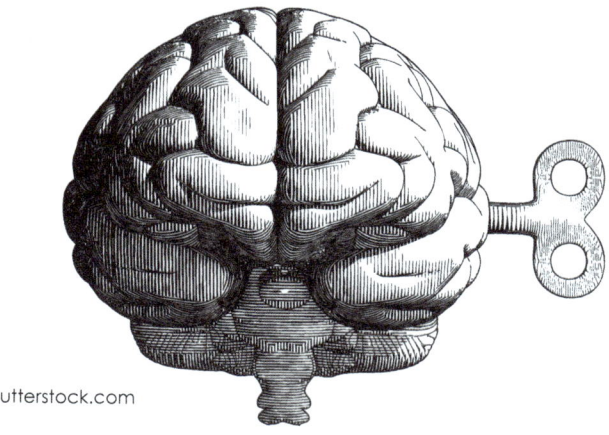

© Jolygon/Shutterstock.com

A common finding in these studies is the high levels of both dopamine and norepinephrine.

Dopamine is commonly known as the pleasure chemical, but more accurately it is the *anticipation* of pleasure chemical. Dopamine levels rise when we are eating a chocolate bar, but dopamine levels are at their highest level *before* we eat the chocolate bar and are looking forward to it. It is the anticipation of a reward that causes these levels to spike. Rewards may be physical, emotional, psychological, etc.

Dopamine

© Anastasiya Litvinenka/Shutterstock.com

Norepinephrine, or noradrenaline, is known as the danger chemical. It rises in tandem with the body's response to stress or perceived threat.

When these two chemicals coexist, attention is at its highest point. The juxtaposition of a potential reward and a potential threat focuses our thoughts like a laser.

NOREPINEPHRINE

© khuntapol/Shutterstock.com

Imagine that your boss says that he has 100-dollar bills to give away to the first three people who respond correctly to his trivia questions. If you are like most people, you will instantly give the boss your full attention, fueled by the anticipation of a possible reward and simultaneously, the potential threat of losing out to a colleague. Your concentration will be so great that you will ignore an incoming message on your phone, ignore people moving around the room, ignore your own internal distractions.

If we know which chemicals, or neurotransmitters are at play naturally, during episodes of heightened attention, we may also work backward to create focused attention at will. By designing a situation which promises a potential reward while also threatening a potential loss, we can ensure the production of desired neurotransmitters and our listeners will experience focused attention.

Retaining Attention

While humans enjoy familiarity because it gives them a sense of security and comfort, our brains are hardwired to pay attention to novelty.

Novelty

Imagine sitting in a crowded coffee shop with a friend. People are constantly walking by, yet none of them draw your attention away from your friend. You are able to contribute to the conversation with little distraction. If, however, out of the corner of your eye you see a man wearing full body armor chances are that your attention will immediately be drawn to him. His presence is novel and unexpected (raising your dopamine) while setting your threat antenna to high alert (raising norepinephrine) in case he poses a danger.

An element of novelty is crucial when choosing a speech topic. People are much more likely to pay attention when a topic is unique and unfamiliar to them, yet made relevant. (More on relevance in the chapter entitled *Inform*.) It may also suffice to simply offer a different perspective on a familiar topic. Either way, novelty is key.

Pattern Interrupts

© Elena11/Shutterstock.com

Using novelty is a way to continually gain attention throughout a presentation. The reason that novelty gains our interest is because it interrupts an expected pattern.

For example, if a speaker says:

Monday, Tuesday, Wednesday, Thursday, Friday, Saturday....

You expect the next word to be Sunday. If instead the speaker says *but Sunday never came,* it breaks the expected pattern and gains your attention.

Incorporating pattern interrupts into your speaking will ensure that you keep the audience mentally alert and engaged.

Once we have people's attention, it is important to use that attention wisely.

Immediately after using a pattern interrupt, include important data that you want the audience to recall.

Remember: Attention is a limited resource.

Audience Engagement

Another way to facilitate audience attention is to engage with your listeners. While it is essential to engage with them throughout, we can use engagement in a particular way to reinforce our data. When a listener actively, rather than passively, engages with your data, they are much more likely to recall it.

It is common knowledge that people learn from hands-on activities due to active participation, but what is less well known, is that "hands-on" can be "mind-on." Having a listener mentally participate in an activity has the same effect.

For example, compare the communication of a piece of data:

Without engagement:

The War of 1812 was a conflict between the US and the UK. (Dry, boring fact)

With engagement:

What countries have gone to war with the US?

(Responses may be: Afghanistan, Vietnam, etc.)

What about English-speaking countries? Can anyone think of one? (This changes the way we think about the question and requires active mental participation)

Whether or not the audience was previously aware of this war, they will think about it actively with this conversation. Active thinking leads to recall.

Everyday Conversation Practice:

1. **Try combining a possible reward and a possible threat in an everyday conversation. i.e.** *Oh, I could really go for yam rolls at that great new sushi place tonight. How about you?* (Possible reward) *We better book right now because it's hard to get a reservation on the weekends.* (Possible threat)
2. **Try using a pattern interrupt in a conversation.** When someone is expecting you to say something particular, or respond in a particular way - mix it up. Surprise them. Interrupt the pattern.

Data Overload is Dangerous

Have you ever spent a couple of hours listening to a class lecture, walked out of the room and had a conversation that goes something like this?

Your Friend Bob:
Man, I'm spent. That was exhausting.

You:
Yeah. I was totally paying attention but I have no idea what she said.

Your Friend Bob:
Me neither!

You:
I even have seven pages of notes! I must be stupid or something.

News flash: You're not stupid and it's not your fault. It's called cognitive overload. It's real. It's ugly. And it's avoidable.

Cognitive Load Theory

Cognitive Load Theory suggests that we have a finite capacity to process information at any given moment in time (Chandler and Sweller 1991; Paas, Van Gog, and Sweller 2010). This limitation is a physiological one.

Think of going to the gym, dehydrated, on an empty stomach and attempting to have a great workout. Your body simply doesn't have the resources to produce adequate energy. Though we don't tend to think of mental activity requiring the same resources, the brain does need energy to think, understand and remember.

Another consideration with regard to mental processing is the capacity of short-term or working memory. It is widely understood that we can hold seven items in working memory at one time; beyond seven items, recall becomes difficult.

© Tetyana Snezhyk/Shutterstock.com

Try this:

Read through the list *once*. Then look away and write down the words you remember.

- Bureau
- Recognize
- Chapped
- Triumph
- Carousel
- Prior
- Allude
- Around
- Solidarity
- Hank
- Rotate
- Harness
- Ties
- Chaser
- Whip
- Nair

You might feel like a one-time read through the list didn't give you a fair chance to recall most of the words, but this is also what happens when you hear words or ideas. You have only one chance to comprehend and remember.

Cognitive Load Theory suggests that not only can we process seven items or less at a time, with adequate brain glucose, but that if we overload the brain, it will take its own holiday. More on that later. Let's look at Cognitive Load Theory or CLT:

Each of the blue dots is a piece of information or data: a thought about the weekend, a concern about a relationship, an interesting fact

100 Percent
This is the brain at 100 percent capacity.
© Toponium/Shutterstock.com

about fireflies, seeing and processing a familiar face, hearing and identifying a noise, worrying if the oven is turned off, etc. The possibilities are endless. Each of these bits of data requires brain glucose to process. Each requires mental energy.

This capacity is broken into three components:

Extraneous Load

Intrinsic Load

Germane Load

Extraneous Load

Extraneous Load is made up of existing thoughts, worries and plans.

When a listener enters a room for a class or to hear a presentation, that listener is not a "blank slate."

Let's say you are the presenter. You might be tempted to think along these lines:

I have a lot of information; I am the expert on this topic. People coming to listen to me are like blank slates. I am going to tell them what I know and when they leave the room, they will know what I know.

Sounds reasonable, right? Except that it's not. It's a huge misconception to believe that people will remember everything that you said. It's also a misconception to believe that people have a whole lot of "mental room" to understand and process your information.

Remember the 100 percent capacity? Research shows that when listeners enter a room, they may have 30 percent of that capacity already taken. It is used up by existing thoughts, worries and plans. Someone who is stressed, busy or is running from meeting to meeting might have up to 90 percent of that capacity already taken.

You will never know whether your listener is at 30 or 90 percent, but either way, you know that they are not at 0 percent. Their capacity is already partially full. Keep that in mind as we talk about the other components.

Extraneous load is also responsible for processing the visual part of visual media, such as slides, graphs, charts, etc. This is a little confusing, but it has nothing to do with processing the content on the slides or charts, but the visual pieces like text, numbers, colors, font, images, etc. The content itself will be processed by Intrinsic Load.

(There will be a full discussion on using visual media effectively in the chapter entitled: *Beware of the Competition*.) For now, remember that simply seeing something and paying attention to it requires brain glucose and contributes to total cognitive load.

Before we look at intrinsic and germane load, let's consider this very important fact:

As soon as the brain reaches overload, it stops paying attention to the task at hand and reverts to what we will call for now "daydream" mode, or System 1 processing. This switch of thinking modes is involuntary; we don't choose or recognize the switch.

Think back. Have you ever been paying attention to a presentation and then all of a sudden you realize that you have been daydreaming about your weekend for quite a while?

This is overload in action.

The problem with this departure from paying attention is that we are lost when we finally return to paying attention. We no longer know what the speaker is talking about. We have missed crucial information. This "out of the loop" syndrome demotivates us even more. It's hard to pay attention and play catch up when we're lost. It's hard work and more often than not, we subconsciously decide that it's not worth it and we go back to daydreaming.

This very real possibility—of listeners zoning out of your presentation—is a message killer. People cannot be educated, inspired, or influenced by a message that they didn't hear.

Intrinsic Load

Intrinsic load is the new data received by the listener. This data may include facts, statistics, narratives, etc. The word data is used here to encompass all new information.

Not All Data Is Processed Equally

Data can be divided into hard data and soft data. The brain processes the two types of data differently.

Let's look at which data is considered hard and which is considered soft; then we will discuss why it matters.

Hard Data

Facts

Numerical Data
(Stats, Equations, Ratios, etc.)

Visual Media

Soft Data

Narratives
(Personal Stories, Business Stories)

Anecdotes

Analogies
(+ All Literary Devices)

Examples
(Data with a Human Face)

Descriptions

Questions:
(Actual, Rhetorical, Socratic)

Humor
simple image (exception)
music

Why Does It Matter?

While it is difficult to measure quantitatively, it has been suggested that it takes 7× more brain glucose to process hard data than it does to process soft data.

This means that that the Intrinsic Load bucket fills 7× more quickly when the speaker uses hard data versus soft data. In other words, as a speaker, you have the power to control how the audience pays attention. Many presentations look like this:

Fact

Fact

Fact

Fact

Statistic

Ratio

Chart

Graph

Fact

Busy Slide

Busy Slide

Etc.

So much hard data back-to-back is mentally exhausting for the listener.

There is a simple, yet not widely known solution which requires speakers to be very intentional about their information management.

Information Management

The average listener can process approximately seven minutes worth of continuous hard data before reaching mental exhaustion and needing replenishment of brain glucose.

A conscientious speaker will avoid overloading listeners by taking two steps:

1. Limiting the use of hard data.
2. Spacing the hard data throughout the presentation.

These two steps may be accomplished by using a data ratio of 4:1 soft: hard.

4:1

Soft: Hard

In other words, for every piece of hard data you use in an oral presentation, you should use four pieces of soft data. This may sound impossible, especially if you are in an industry which relies heavily on hard data. It's not impossible, nor is it difficult.

It simply means using an example after seven minutes worth of facts, or inserting a quick humorous comment in the middle of a series of equations. The good news is that the brain only needs a thirty-second break to relax and allow the brain glucose to replenish itself, in order to be ready for another seven minutes worth of hard data.

Another way to manage hard data, is to change hard data to soft data. This is called

re-framing the data.

Here is an example:

Seventy-eight percent is a statistic, which would qualify as hard data.

By simply re-framing the 78 percent as an example, we are now using soft data.

An example might be:

Seventy-eight percent of Apple's revenue comes from...... etc.

By putting a human face on the number, it becomes an example and therefore, soft data.

Soft data are easier to process and intuitively preferred by the audience.

Soft data are also processed in such a way that allows acceptance without skepticism. We will discuss that in greater detail when we discuss Systems of Thinking.

You will be surprised at how much easier it is to hold your audience's attention when you manage your data.

EXTRANEOUS + INTRINSIC + GERMANE = 100%

Germane Load

Germane load is where retention takes place. In order for a listener to recall information there has to be space available in Germane Load.

Retention takes place when a speaker has available mental capacity and has time to process the new information at the time of learning. In order to facilitate retention, we can remember two things:

1. Avoid overloading the audience with hard data. Use the data ratio above, ideally, or at least manage the amount of hard data you include. When possible, either give small breaks by using soft data, or re-frame some hard data as soft data. Space the hard data apart to reduce listener fatigue.

2. When delivering new information, give the listener time to reflect on it, before continuing to speak. Most of the time, listeners are so busy trying to keep up with the speaker that they fail to incorporate or learn the new information. Using a pause in your speaking allows the listener to take the new information, and associate with something they already know, thereby forming a mental schema. This mental schema puts the new information in a mental drawer, where the listener can find it later. When we don't know where to look for something, we can't find it.

Schemas Are Formed

Here is an example of germane load, used well, to form a schema:

Speaker:

Did you know that 42 percent of companies selling x lost money last year?
Pause. (Allows the listener to process the information)

Speaker:

42 percent%!
(Uses repetition, which will reinforce the new information.)
That means 42 out of every 100 companies lost money last year.
(Re-framing by changing the 42 from a statistic to an example or changing from hard to soft data format, while retaining the same idea)

Listener:

(Thinking to himself)

42 percent? Wow. That's higher than I thought it would be.

Later that week if the listener tries to recall what the speaker said about companies losing money it is likely, that with the repetition, he will recall the number 42. If not, because he has formed a schema, he knows where to look for that information. (*I remember it was higher than I expected... what was it.... oh right, 42 percent.*)

Cognitive Processing: Dual Process Theory

In order to comprehend how messages are cognitively processed, it is useful to examine dual process theories. Early theorists established the idea that there are two distinct processes of thought, a central, or consciously cognitive process and an unconscious or peripheral route (James 1884.) Richard Petty and John Cacioppo (1986) call these routes central processing and peripheral processing. Central route processing involves active cognitive participation by the listener. Peripheral processing occurs when focus is on peripheral cues such as speaker attractiveness rather than on message substance.

In Tversky and Kahneman's Systems 1 and 2 dual process theory (1981), System 2 is the slower, more deliberate, and analytical cognitive system while System 1 is the faster, intuitive emotional system. While System 2 has often been perceived to be the "leader" in earlier dual process theories, Kahneman suggests that this is false and that System 1 is the default system, only requiring the assistance of System 2 when necessary. His research suggests that there is no evidence for simultaneous processing and that one system or the other is at work (Kahneman 2011).

It would be exhausting to be in System 2 continuously, due to the amount of physical and mental energy required; therefore, we are not in System 2 unless we need to be.

Chip and Dan Heath in the book *Switch,* offer a helpful image to remember the different systems. System 1 can be compared to an elephant (large, powerful) while System 2 is the rider (more analytical but less powerful). We all know who is in control when it comes to an elephant and a rider!

Let's compare the Systems:

System 1 (The Elephant)

Quick

Requires little effort

Intuitive

Emotional

Habitual

System 2 (The Rider)

Slow

Deliberate

Analytical

Rational

Requires considerable effort

Exhausting

Generally speaking, System 1 is in charge of unconscious and sub-conscious behavior, movement, emotional reactions, habits, and "easy thinking". When we listen to a story, we are actively thinking but not concentrating in the same way as when we listen to the delivery of hard data. This is why we resort to System 1 when we experience cognitive fatigue.

© MaxNadya/Shutterstock.com

Processing often depends upon content, but it also depends upon our personal experiences.

For example:

We think of math equations as a System 2 activity, requiring slow deliberate thought. This would be true if you were asked to process the equation 24,702 multiplied by 966.

However, if you are asked to calculate 2 + 2, you don't need System 2 because you know the answer, based on mental habits.

Similarly, we can look at golf. If you are new to the sport, for you, golf may be a System 2 activity. You have to remember to hold the club correctly, adopt the proper stance, keep your head down, follow through on your swing, etc. A great deal of concentration is necessary. For Bob, who is a pro golfer, these things are habit; he can do them in his sleep. For Bob, golf is a System 1 activity. If Bob gets nervous at a tournament, when the stakes are high, he may overthink his swing and resort to System 2 thinking. This is where even pro athletes can get into trouble. Bob is a good System 1 golfer, but now he has switched to a system which doesn't allow him to use his instincts.

The Heuristic Systematic Model of processing (Chaiken 1980; Chaiken and Eagly 1976) proposes the **sufficiency principle**, which suggests that listeners desire to receive a sufficient amount of information to reach a decision, neither more, nor less.

We only need and want what is sufficient. More is not better; it is just exhausting.

By helping our listeners remain in System 1, whenever possible, we are preventing cognitive overload and mental fatigue. Guiding them into System 2 when necessary will ensure that they have the resources to process complex information when it matters most.

Everyday Conversation Practice

In the context of an everyday conversation:

1. **Manage Your Data.** Even in conversational speaking, we can overwhelm people with unnecessary information. When we do, they tune out. Think of exactly what information is necessary to make your point. Give no more, no less. With frequent practice, make it a new habit.

2. **Re-Frame Your Data.** Take a fact (hard) and turn it into an example (soft). i.e. Fact: Doodlebugs are endangered. Re-frame as Example: I watched a documentary on doodlebugs and they are disappearing by the thousands every year in East Africa.

Note that the same core information is being conveyed, just in a different form. i.e. Fact: The GDP increased 1.9 % last year. Re-frame as Question: How much do you think the GDP increased last year?

The more you practice the small skills in conversation, the more they become habits. The goal is to form new habits. Once you have good speaking habits, public speaking is easy.

Beware of The Competition

Visual media can be a powerful tool for a speaker, but only if it is used well.

Visual media includes anything from PowerPoint slides, Keynote Slides, Google Slides, Haiku Deck, to photos, diagrams, charts, graphs, videos, etc.

But—SPEAKER BEWARE!!
© Kwaczek/Shutterstock.com
Your visual media can become unwelcome *competition*.

In January 2003, NASA celebrated the successful launch of one of its shuttles Columbia.

It wasn't until the following day, when NASA received external footage of the launch, that they realized that during the ascent "something had hit "somewhere." They didn't know what that something was, nor did they know whether or not this impact posed a significant problem for the shuttle.

NASA requested that their Boeing engineers investigate by looking through the footage frame by frame. What they discovered was that a piece of foam had broken free from the thermal heating tank and impacted the left wing of the aircraft, creating a hole. When they compared their test data with actual event data, they determined that the impact was far beyond test data for the impact to avoid catastrophic damage. In other words, they had a huge problem.

The Boeing engineers prepared twenty-two PowerPoint slides and presented them to the board at NASA. At the end of that presentation, everyone from NASA walked out of the room and sighed a collective sigh of relief. *Close call, but no problem.*

No problem? What happened here?

Every single person in the room missed the key message of this presentation.

How is this possible? It is almost certain that the engineers and members of the board are very intelligent individuals.

Let's look at this slide from *Beautiful Evidence* by Edward Tufte:

Review of Test Data Indicates Conversatism for Tile Penetration

https://www.edwardtufte.com/bboard/q-and-a-fetch-msg?msg_id=0001yB

This is the slide which contains the crucial bit of data—the evidential data are outside of the test data range.

Although you might be able to identify the crucial information on the slide as you are reading it silently to yourself, at your own pace, (especially since you were told what to look for) remember that the people who missed this information were *listening to a speaker while attempting to read and process this slide at the same time*. Therein lies the problem.

The crucial piece of data lies at the very bottom of the slide. This placement itself presents a problem. We don't expect the most important information on a visual to be placed at the bottom of a slide. We don't expect the crucial information to be designated by a small bullet.

We don't expect the crucial information to look exactly the same as all of the other information on the slide.

The problem then, lies in both the design of the slide and the delivery of the slide.

The brain has two separate channels for visual and auditory processing (Mayer and Anderson 1991; Paivio 1991). Unless the data entering from one channel are extremely basic and simple, we cannot process through both channels simultaneously in a meaningful way.

Attention Theory suggests that parallel processing of complex information cannot be executed efficiently (Bergen, Grimes, and Potter 2005). When we try to read complex text and at the same time, listen to a speaker, we experience the **split-attention effect.** What we like to think is multitasking, is instead a quick shift of attention back and forth. Consequently, we are neither listening well, nor reading well. In addition, the split-attention effect imposes a heavy cognitive load.

It is almost always the case that speakers speak more slowly than we can read. Therefore, there is always a disconnect between what we are seeing and what we are hearing.

In order for dual processing to be effective (hearing and seeing at the same time) the information has to match and be delivered in sync. This is related to a theory called **Perceptual Grouping** (Treisman, Kahneman, and Burkell 1983). When we are able to process auditory and visual information simultaneously with success, it is because the content is the same or similar enough to be grouped together in the listener's mind. When this happens, the working memory capacity can in fact be enhanced for the learner.

One working theory, and the opinion of this author based on research and experience, is that *in order for dual processing to be effective, the information coming from visual and auditory channels cannot both require System 2 processing.*

We are able to look at a simple image (System 1 processing) while listening to a speaker explain a concept (System 2). We can read a few phrases (System 2) while listening to music (System 1) but what we cannot do effectively is to process reading sentences (System 2) while simultaneously processing a verbal explanation (Also System 2).

If you are careful in using visual media, your audience attention, comprehension and retention will be markedly better than in most presentations.

Many, many speakers go full tilt with slides and explanations and wonder why the result is death by PowerPoint.

© Alexander_P/Shutterstock.com

Why Use Visual Media

While it seems obvious, the first question to ask is **Do I need visual media?**

There should always be a purpose in using visual media in a presentation, due to the increased cognitive load that it presents. Using visual media should not be the default setting. You do not need a slide for everything you say.

There are only three good reasons for using visual media in a presentation:

1. It helps to clarify a concept.
2. It makes a concept memorable.
3. It signposts the speaker's place in the presentation.

Clarifying a Concept

If a diagram would make it easier for the audience to understand your idea, then use the diagram. Do not use a diagram or picture just to decorate a slide. We don't need to see a picture of a giraffe just because you are mentioning giraffes. Remember that speakers have to make different decisions than writers.

Making a Concept Memorable

If your audience will remember your idea after the presentation because you have created a memorable image which communicates that idea, then use the image. If not, skip it.

Signposting

Signposting slides have a single purpose and that is to remind the audience exactly where they are in the course of your presentation. If you have seven steps in a process, on which you are elaborating throughout the talk, it may be helpful for your audience to see a slide saying:

Step 3. This way, they can mentally follow along and know what to expect as you proceed.

If you do decide to use visual media, follow the design principles below.

Simplicity, Simplicity, Simplicity

The secret to using visual media effectively is simplicity.

1. **Diagrams, charts, graphs, slides,** etc., should be as simple and basic as possible. In order to facilitate this, ask yourself: What is the point of this visual? What is the idea I am trying to communicate? Then use a **preattentive visual attribute** to emphasize this point. (See below). What else is necessary in this visual? If it's not necessary, delete it.
2. **Text**: When using text, abide by the **4×4 Rule**. Never use more than four words across on a slide or chart and never use more than four rows of text in a vertical

direction. 4×4 should be a *maximum*. The more complex the text, the less text you should use per slide. Remember that text is not a great visual choice because it fails to maximize the visual medium. We cannot look at text and immediately comprehend an idea, in the same way that we can with a photo.

Processing of text requires analytical thinking.

You may have heard that you should avoid having too many slides, but this should not be a concern. It doesn't matter how many slides you have; the content of each single slide matters. It would be better to have more slides with less content on each slide.

Note: Notice the lack of simplicity and the lack of preattentive visual attributes in the NASA slide.

Preattentive Visual Attributes

Our eye is drawn to novelty. Regardless of content, the eye first pays attention to what stands out from the rest.

See the images below.

Our eye is drawn immediately to the yellow face and to the blue paint.

© BeeBright/Shutterstock.com

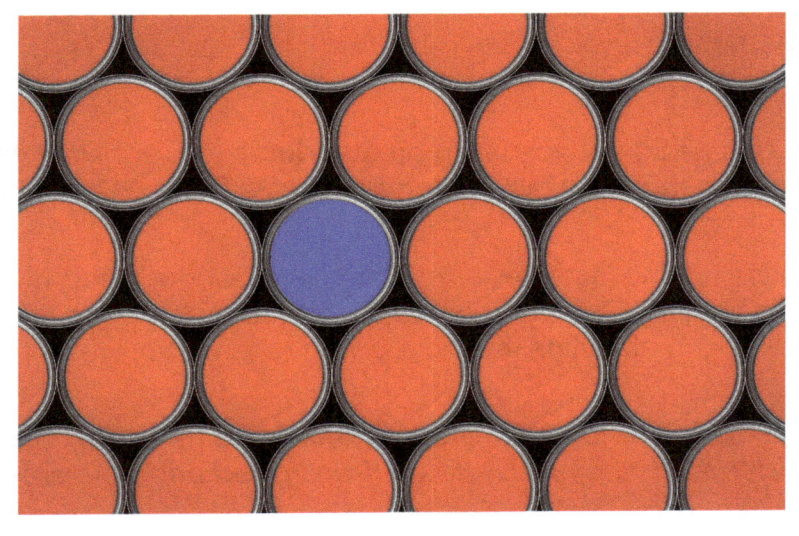

© Phonlamai Photo/Shutterstock.com

Four Attributes:

    Color

    Form

    Spatial Positioning

    Movement

By adding a preattentive attribute to a slide, diagram, or chart, we can ensure that we control exactly where the audience is looking and therefore control their attention.

Designing a Visual and Using Preattentive Visual Attributes:

https://medium.com/analytics-vidhya/how-every-data-set-deserves-to-be-told-better-into-a-story-cb5ff4874f0c

A Surprising Winner?

Studies have been conducted to determine which visuals have the greatest impact on listeners. The result may surprise you. Listeners reported that being dazzled by professional slide decks and moving graphics was neither the most effective for recall, nor did it provide the most powerful, memorable experience. What did they choose instead? Live hand drawings.

A speaker who draws a diagram while speaking and explaining is engaging the audience through the visual medium rather than showing the audience a stagnant image. The audience joins the discovery process and consequently, pays greater attention and recalls ideas with greater accuracy.

Not the greatest artist? Apparently, it doesn't matter. Anyone can draw basic shapes and lines and that's all you need! If you're interested in improving your skills in basic drawing, *The Back of the Napkin* and *Show & Tell* both by Dan Roam, are helpful resources for this purpose.

Here's a quick tutorial with Dan:

How to Draw Anything:

https://youtu.be/-3tV9E00N20

If you're interested in design principles in greater depth, a worthwhile recommendation is Google's Cole Nussbaumer Knaflic in *Storytelling with Data: A Data Visualization Guide for Business Professionals.*

If you work with visualizing data on a regular basis, a good read is *How to Lie with Statistics*, a classic book by Darrell Huff, that discusses simple but serious mistakes that people make when using statistics, especially with regard to representing statistics in a visual manner.

The bottom line is to remember that visuals should be used only after careful, conscientious consideration; they must be well-designed and delivered with caution.

Beware of the competition.

Big Idea: Beware of The Competition

EVERYDAY CONVERSATION PRACTICE:
1. Practice illustrating everyday explanations with simple drawings. Draw on the back of a napkin!
2. Practice designing simple slides, using preattentive visual attributes so that when you need to design for an upcoming presentation, you will have developed good habits. Ask others for feedback on your slide. Is the point clear? Are there unnecessary details?
3. Try re-designing the NASA slide to make it effective. Show it to someone in conversation and ask them to identify the point of the slide. Fun fact: Nasa has since banned PowerPoint presentations. This drastic step is not necessary. We just have to be intentional and use the software effectively.

Strategy is Surefire

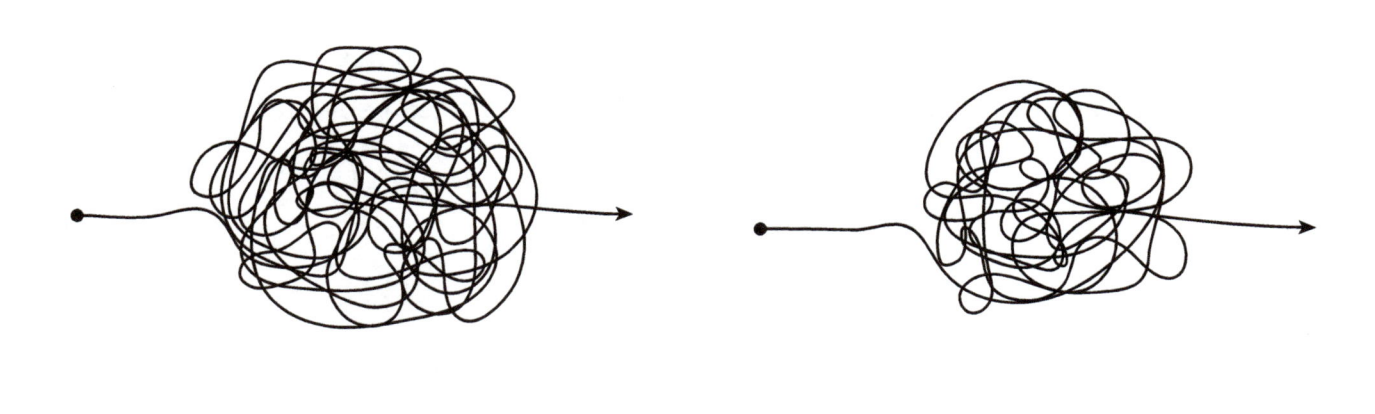

Without strategy, we are left untangling abstract mental concepts and trying to translate them into words. Strategy is a savior for speakers.

The strategy itself will depend on the speaking purpose. The following seven chapters are organized by purpose. Each purpose has its own strategy or strategies. As with anything, practice is the key to success. The more familiar the strategies become, the easier they are to use and the more effective your speaking becomes.

While it seems an obvious statement, the following point is often neglected:

All great speaking begins with intentional thinking.
© Rachel Rofe/Shutterstock.com

It's impossible to give a great talk, or to influence others when your own ideas are not clear. Intentional thinking takes both effort and time, but it is well worth it.

While we will give some purpose-specific guidelines in the chapters that follow, here is a general list of questions to consider at the initial phase of creating a message.

FIRST CONSIDERATIONS

*What is my general purpose? (To inform, to persuade, to entertain, etc.)

*Who is my audience?

*What do they already know about this topic?

*Will I be the true expert in the room?

*Are they attending my presentation voluntarily or is it a requirement?

*What is their expectation of me/my message?

*Where will the delivery of this message take place?

*When will it take place?

*Will my audience be "fresh" or exhausted?

*What is the tone of the event? (Formal, casual, etc.)

*What do I want my audience to do after hearing my message?

*Is there a predetermined time limit?

*Can I reasonably accomplish this goal within the time that I have to speak?

*If not, how do I choose what to eliminate?

*Which ideas must I communicate, without fail?

*Which ideas are optional to communicate?

*What kind of examples would best serve this audience?

*How do I ensure that I deliver a manageable amount of data?

*Do I think I may need visual media?

*How can I engage this particular audience?

*How can I think outside the box to communicate my ideas?

Pay attention to the answers. They may change as you go through the process, but at this early stage they will help to point you in a specific direction.

Once this initial brainstorming is complete, find a map to help with planning.

GAB LAB: The Playbook of Public Speaking Prowess Through Everyday Conversation

A map may be **visual** or **mental:**

© Andrey_Popov/Shutterstock.com

© magic pictures/Shutterstock.com

© rSnapshotPhotos/Shutterstock.com

© JustDOne/Shutterstock.com

Maps help in four ways:

1. Maps help the speaker to structure ideas logically and meaningfully.
2. Maps help a speaker differentiate between speaking purposes and organize accordingly.
3. Maps help the speaker to assist the audience in understanding by packaging ideas for recall and retention.
4. Maps help a speaker visualize their ideas and deliver conversationally with big picture recall. Whether a map is written or visualized mentally, it should maximize the visual medium to encourage recall. Principles of maximizing the visual medium are discussed at length in the chapter entitled *Beware of the Competition.*

Strategies, maps and templates all assist a speaker by the structural organization they offer, but also in the knowledge that a plan exists. This can reduce public speaking anxiety significantly.

Use a brainstorming map to get ideas flowing, then find the appropriate map for your speaking purpose. (See Respond, Inform, Persuade, Entertain chapters)

Once you know the map for each purpose, you will always have a plan and effective speaking will become a habit.

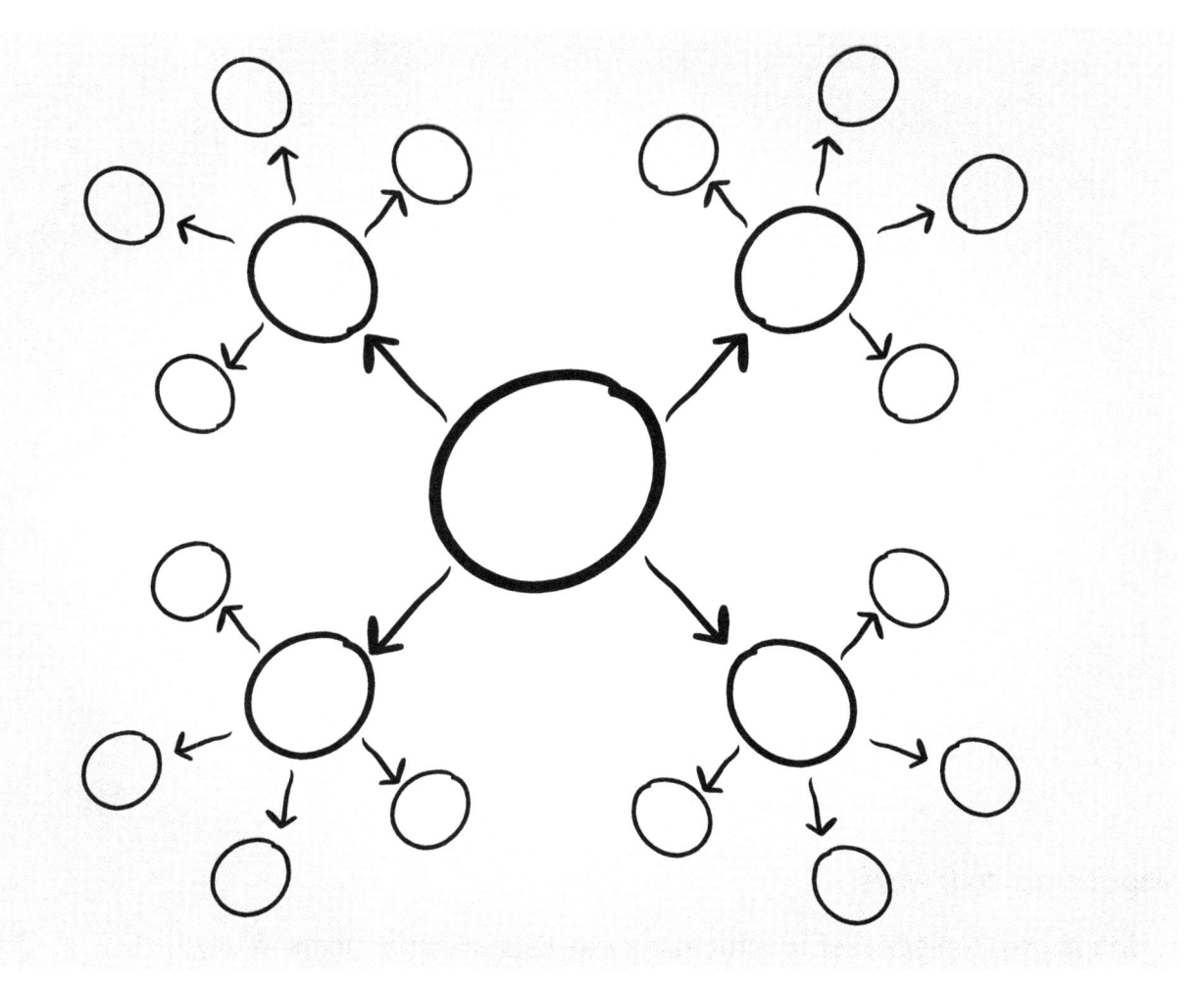

GAB LAB: The Playbook of Public Speaking Prowess Through Everyday Conversation

© KindheartedStock/Shutterstock.com

Big Idea: Strategy is Surefire

Everyday (Conversation) Practice:

Throughout the subsequent chapters, there will be numerous opportunities to use specific maps designed for specific purposes.
In the meantime, try using a map for each of the following everyday scenarios:

1. **Brainstorm an idea.** Print and use the MindMap template to elaborate on an idea for a project, a paper, a vacation. This may seem like a basic and overly simplistic exercise, but it is the key to clear and creative thinking.

2. **Brainstorm a conversation.** Then have the conversation.

Connect

© Zarja/Shutterstock.com

Here is the secret to forging connections.

The Story of One Woman, Two Men and Two Dinners:

https://www.goodreads.com/quotes/1456795-in-the-torrid-london-summer-of-1886-william-gladstone-was

Disraeli had mastered the art of connection.

Historically, there has been a debate in the field of oration. Debaters argued which qualities were the most important in a successful speaker: great messaging or a great delivery. Clearly both are important, but they wanted to identify which was most important.

The debate was tricky to resolve—until recently.

Due to the advent of fMRI scans and PET scans, we can now measure brain activity in real time. We can measure human reactions and see how they translate to the development of thoughts as well as behaviors.

Even a few years ago, before the technology existed, we relied heavily on self-reporting to explain human behavior and motivation. If you had purchased a car from a dealership and were asked why you had chosen that particular dealership from which to make your purchase, you would have justified your decision with what you thought was a logical reason. We know now, however, that this reason may not have been accurate. You may have made an emotional decision and rationalized it after the fact.

For example, imagine that you wanted to purchase a brand new silver Toyota Land Cruiser. You visit three separate dealerships and look at the same model at each respective dealership. The features of all the vehicles are almost identical, with perhaps an added feature here or there, perhaps a slight variation in price. Logic would dictate that you would purchase the vehicle which had all the features you desired and which was offered at the best deal. Interestingly, however, the research shows something else. It shows that overwhelmingly, people will buy the vehicle from the salesperson *with whom they forged the strongest connection.*

Does it make sense to buy a car from someone just because you like them, when you will probably never see them again? It's not rational, but we don't always make rational decisions. Many people when they hear this, exclude themselves from such irrational decision-making. *Oh I would never do that*. Apparently, however, this kind of decision-making is very common.

When we feel a connection with someone, we are more likely to accept their message. We are much more likely to take a recommendation from a friend, than from a data-reliable source or study. The power of connection is undeniable.

How then do we go about forging connections?

How to Forge Connections

Eye Contact

The first and most obvious way to forge connections is through authentic eye contact. As mentioned in the chapter called *Impressions Matter,* one thought, one person is the ideal manner of establishing eye contact with an audience of more than one.

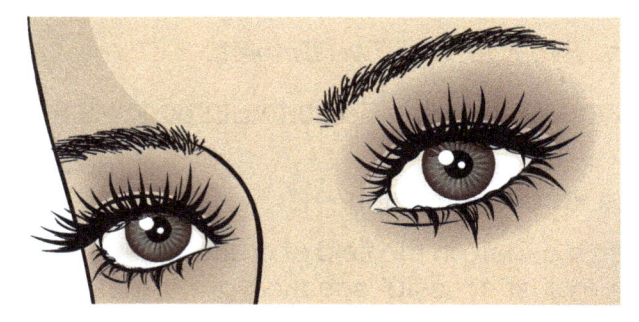

Studies have found that sustained eye contact is a key indicator in deep, meaningful human connection.
© Tetiana Dickens/Shutterstock.com

A study conducted by Cornell University (Tal, Musicus, and Wansink 2014) is just one of many studies which have looked at how eye contact produces a subconscious sense of connection. In this study, adults preferred boxes of cereal which featured a cartoon rabbit making eye contact with the viewer, over similar boxes where the rabbit was instead featured looking away.

A study by Kinsey-Goman (2011) found that we perceive speakers who do not make eye contact as less prepared, uneasy and insincere.

Again, it is worth mentioning that these norms are expected and appreciated within a large sector of Western society, but that there are exceptions within specific Indigenous bands and other ethnic groups. We must be mindful of these differences and be certain to respect them accordingly.

Think of Drawing People "Out"

As Disraeli demonstrated, an effective way to establish connection is to draw people out of themselves. Generally speaking, people like to talk about themselves; they like to share their opinions, experiences and thoughts. The more someone feels respected and valued, the more they will share and the more quickly a connection can be forged. In order for this to work successfully, we need to demonstrate a *genuine interest* in the person who is speaking.

Remember that we can learn something from anyone, regardless of diverse backgrounds and perspectives. Instead of allowing ourselves to become divided on issues where we differ in opinion, use this technique instead.

© studiostoks/Shutterstock.com

Curiosity Card

Let's say you meet Bob for the first time and he tells you that he consumes insects on a regular basis because of their high protein content.

What you might feel like saying:

Are you insane? That sounds disgusting. Are you some kind of freak?

If you say that, however, you and Bob will never forge a connection. The relationship will be over before it begins. You might miss out on a fantastic friendship; first impressions are not always correct.

Instead, say something that demonstrates your fascination with this unique perspective. Do not demonstrate disgust, or anger, rather demonstrate curiosity.

Really? Insects? Wow. That is so interesting! Tell me Bob, I'm curious what made you want to try that? Tell me about it.

Here, you are respecting Bob, respecting Bob's opinions (without having to accept them as your own) and very likely learning something new in the process. Education requires us to be exposed to new perspectives, not simply rejecting anything that is discrepant to our own viewpoints.

On a similar note, remember that people do not hold divergent perspectives in order to make you angry. They hold diverse views because they have different backgrounds and they have had different experiences. Remember that we are equal and that everyone has a right to their opinion. We don't have to agree with everything, but we should be respectful listeners.

Rather than allowing discord to prevail, have a **sense of humor**. Humor can save the day.

Empathetic Feedback

Brothers and co-writers Rom and Ori Brafman in their book *Click,* explain the psychology behind human connections and identify tactics to help forge these connections.

Not surprisingly, vulnerability is identified as a powerful tactic. We only truly know someone when they reveal themselves to us. Vulnerability is a way to fast-track this intimacy. When we are willing to share our humanness, others will reciprocate.

A natural bond forms when two or more people share some kind of adversity or struggle. The strongest form of this occurs when the individuals share a common experience. For example, spending a survival weekend with a bunch of strangers is almost guaranteed to transform those strangers into friends or at least allies. A similar bond forms when we discover that someone has had an experience which we also have had. For example, if your mother passed away recently and your colleague's mother also passed away recently, you will form a connection based on shared adversity.

Proximity refers to nearness, with regard to physical space. We are most likely to befriend someone in a class when they sit beside us. This is self-evident, yet we often don't pay attention to our own choices and how they could affect us in the future. If you want to hang out with smart people, choose to sit beside them!

© Yana Tomashova/Shutterstock.com

Proximity for a public speaker means that we are more likely to connect with our audience when we minimize the physical gap between us. A difference of two feet can make a significant impact. There is an energy in the room when we come close to the audience. Standing at the back of the room, behind a podium, is the opposite of proximity; this is yet another reason to avoid this position.

The layout of space matters. Use proximity even if you have to make some surprising choices in arranging a room. Avoid speaking at the head of a large board room table, for example, where some listeners are a football field away. Stand instead at the side of the table so your audience is spread out in greater width than in depth.

Speaker's Position

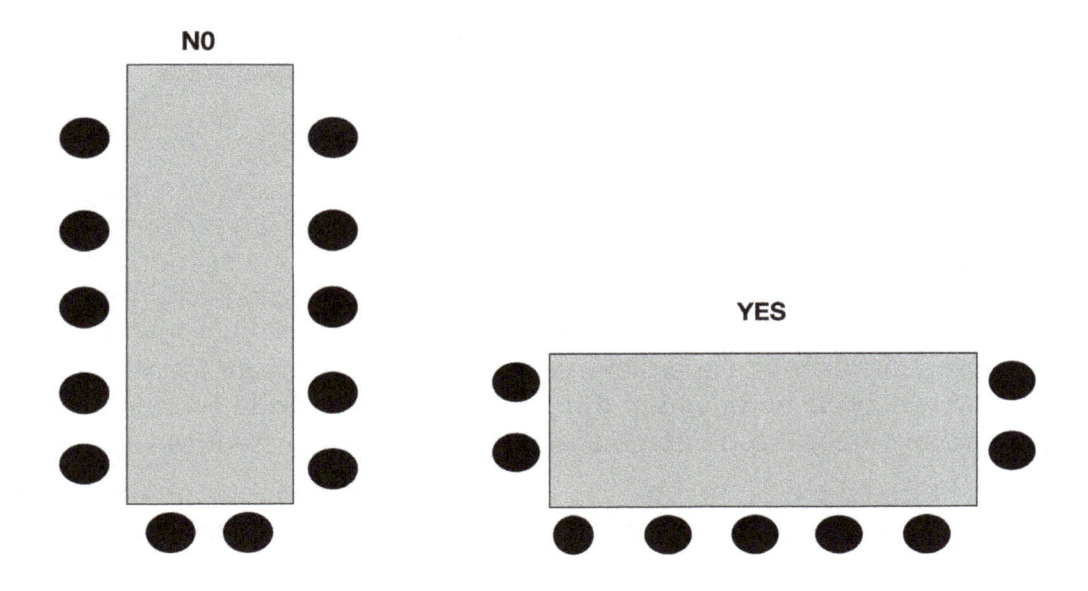

The principle of **similarity** suggests that we like people who are similar to ourselves. This principle is intuitive and easy to put into practice. As a tactic, it means that we should not only enjoy the similarities we share with other people, but make a concentrated effort to discover similarities especially in those toward whom we are not as naturally drawn. This is a good time to remember that as diverse as we are as human beings, we are more similar than different.

As speakers we can find ways to connect with an audience through our commonalities. This requires doing your homework before you speak.

Another way to use similarity is to place yourself on the same level as your audience. Authority is already established when you are in front of the room; you don't need to lord it over people. Speak as an equal rather than as an authority and you will earn respect.

Synchronicity is a fascinating way to forge connections. In our closest relationships, we engage in natural synchronized communication. We subconsciously mimic one another's physical actions, gestures, body posturing, facial expressions, vocal tone and vocal expressions. It's like a dance that neither party realizes they are doing!

Similar to the neural mirroring that happens in storytelling, the brains of the two communicators synchronize which deepens empathy and cooperation.

© Alexey Marcov/Shutterstock.com

By mirroring deliberately and consciously, we can attain the same results. In doing so, we can accelerate connections that would otherwise take a longer period of time to develop if left to natural devices. Mirroring can be done for thirty seconds at the outset of an interaction to forge a connection or to deepen an existing one. Try it. If your friend leans forward in a chair, wait a few seconds and lean forward. If your friend picks up his coffee cup, wait a few seconds and pick up your coffee cup. If your friend laughs loudly, do the same. You may be surprised at the fact that people hardly ever notice what you are doing because it does happen organically in regular circumstances.

No one wants to be fake and the practice is certainly not being encouraged here. This synchronous behavior is only used for the first thirty seconds to one minute of an interaction. The purpose is to make the listener comfortable quickly, so he can be his best, most authentic self. You are doing him a favor. In turn, once you are both comfortable, connections happen easily.

Some people seem to be good at practicing synchronicity. While for some it may come naturally, for others it may be acquired through practice. People who regularly adapt their behavior in a context by matching the tone, energy, volume or physical actions of a speaker or situation are called **high self-monitors.**

Meeting new people does not need to be an awkward experience. Make an effort. Respect your listener and make them feel important. Realize that all people are unique and that you can learn from everyone. You won't become best friends with everyone you meet, but you can have civil, pleasant conversations and make stronger connections every day.

Remember, when speaking in public, we are simply forging connections on a large scale.

> **EVERYDAY CONVERSATION PRACTICE:**
> 1. Focus on making your listener feel important. Draw them out.
> 2. Experiment with vulnerability. See how it changes the dynamic of a conversation.
> 3. Look for similarities between yourself and a new acquaintance, especially one with whom you think you have little in common. Focus the conversation on the similarities and note the positive change in interaction.
> 4. Next time you are in a coffee shop, try using synchronicity to build new connections quickly or to strengthen existing ones.
> 5. When you disagree with someone, try playing the curiosity card.

Connection Cheat Sheet

Peaceful, respectful interaction is necessary to forge connections:

Visualize connection as passing an olive branch.

Think of it as a

"Dove Pass"

© VectorFlower/Shutterstock.com

Draw Them Out
One thought, One Person
Vulnerability
Empathetic Listening

Proximity
Adversity
Similarity
Synchronicity

Respond

Miss South Carolina
Answers a Question
https://youtu.be/lj3iNxZ8Dww

It is easy for any one of us to fail to represent ourselves at our best when we are unprepared to speak.

Certainly, Miss South Carolina is an individual who deserves respect and dignity. No one deserves to be belittled. This video is not included with the intention of being critical, but with the intent to show that having a strategy is essential.

The temptation for most of us, when we are asked a question on the spot, is to open our mouths and immediately begin to speak. While this generally works well for us in conversation, when a question is unexpected, complex, or novel, **we need time to process our *thoughts* before those thoughts are made public.**

Due to the impromptu nature of responding to questions, there may be a misconception that there is no time for us to think and that speaking straight away is the only unfortunate option.

This however, is untrue. In the space between hearing a question and responding to it, we need thinking time. This time may be only ten seconds, but surprisingly, that time is sufficient to choose, plan and structure ideas. Let's call this **The MAGIC 10**.

Let's compare responding without a strategy and with a strategy:

Without a Strategy

Question: What are your thoughts about Politician Dave?

Response: *Well, I mean I don't really like Dave and I don't think he is a great representative—(realizing that wasn't a great thing to say, so now trying to backtrack)—I mean, I'm sure he's a nice guy, but he really cut funding to postsecondary education and that was annoying. Also he makes faces on TV that bug me and he never really seems prepared when he's interviewed, I mean well, except for that one time, you know, during the election interview.......bla bla bla.*

When we don't have a plan, we simply do a quick mental search to come up with anything that seems related to the question. The problem with this approach is that our information is not conveyed in a logical form and we end up sounding a little less intelligent than we probably are.

There's a sense of panic that occurs when someone is waiting for our reply. We feel like we should say something, so we say anything at all. In the worst-case scenario, we say something that we regret. It's easier to avoid making that mistake than it is to fix it!

The better approach is to use a strategy. As mentioned in the *Strategy Is Surefire* chapter, there are two advantages: The first is that knowing that we *have* a strategy removes a lot of the anxiety around worrying about what we might say. The second advantage is that the strategy itself offers a template for organizing and visualizing thoughts.

With a Strategy

© Viktoriia_M/Shutterstock.com

Strategy

Question: What are your thoughts about Politician Dave?

Response:

This time, you will take **THE MAGIC 10**. In that space of time, you will follow this process:

Ask yourself two questions:

1. What is the quick, one sentence answer to the question? (This will become the Core Message)
2. If I shared that answer, what additional information would my listener want to know?

For example:

1. The quick answer is: *I don't think Dave was an effective representative.*
2. A listener would ask WHY, therefore, I need to communicate two reasons: *Economic Policies* and *Public Persona*.

Now, ten seconds are up.

Time to speak.

This time, the response looks like this:

I don't believe that Dave was an effective representative, for two main reasons: his economic policies and his public persona.

This process is easy to follow when you mentally visualize the message map.

Visualize the Message Map.

Message Map

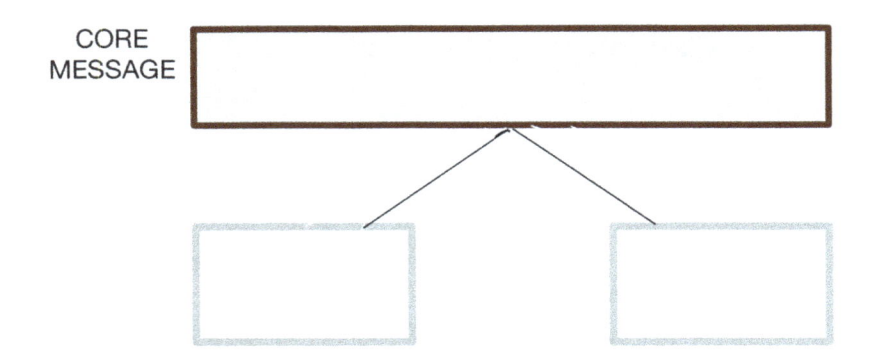

```
                    ┌─────────────────────────────┐
       CORE         │                             │
       MESSAGE      │                             │
                    └─────────────────────────────┘
                              ╱        ╲
                        ┌─────────┐  ┌─────────┐
                        │         │  │         │
                        └─────────┘  └─────────┘
```

You may have heard the public speaking mantra: *tell them what you're going to tell them, tell them, then tell them what you've told them.* This does not always hold true, but it holds true here. Hint: This is great for informative speaking, but not for persuasive speaking.

The process is simple: think, give an overview, elaborate on ideas, review.

Think

Give an Overview

Elaborate

Review

Think: Take the **MAGIC 10**

Overview: I don't believe that Dave was an effective representative, for two main reasons: his economic policies and his public persona.

Elaborate: Go back and give details about the economic policies; when you are finished speaking about that point, move to elaborating on the second point, public persona.

Then, review your points. *In summary, I don't think Dave was a good representative for these two reasons.* If your talk has been very short, make the review very short. If you spoke for a longer period, your review may take a little longer.

Once you know this basic structure, you can apply it to any question or to any message for which you have not had time to prepare.

The two secondary boxes may be populated by any examples or ideas, but it is helpful to consider them with strategy in mind.

The two boxes may contain simply topics or examples (below) or may use a more specific strategy (see Organizational Strategies below).

CORE MESSAGE | 1 SENTENCE SUMMARY OF MESSAGE

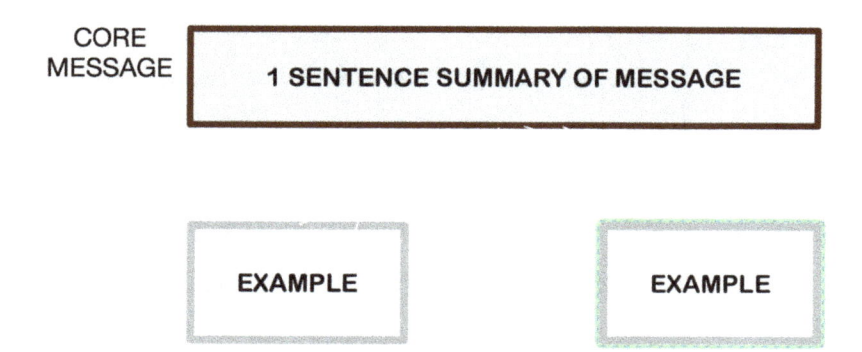

EXAMPLE   EXAMPLE

© Alexander_P/Shutterstock.com

Organizational Strategies

There are a number of specific organizational options we may consider when choosing a strategy. These organizational strategies pertain to the two boxes. Each organizational strategy is followed by a concrete example of how it would be used.

Topical: By topic, or example

Core Message: Domestic pets add value to our lives.

Box I: Dogs   Box 2: Cats

Problem/Solution: Considering first a problem, then a solution

Core Message: Tuition increase is a complex issue.

Box 1: Funding (Problem)   Box 2: Tuition Support (Solution)

```
        CORE
       MESSAGE      ┌─────────────────────────────┐
                    │  1 SENTENCE SUMMARY OF MESSAGE │
                    └─────────────────────────────┘


              ┌───────────┐           ┌───────────┐
              │  PROBLEM  │           │  SOLUTION │
              └───────────┘           └───────────┘
```

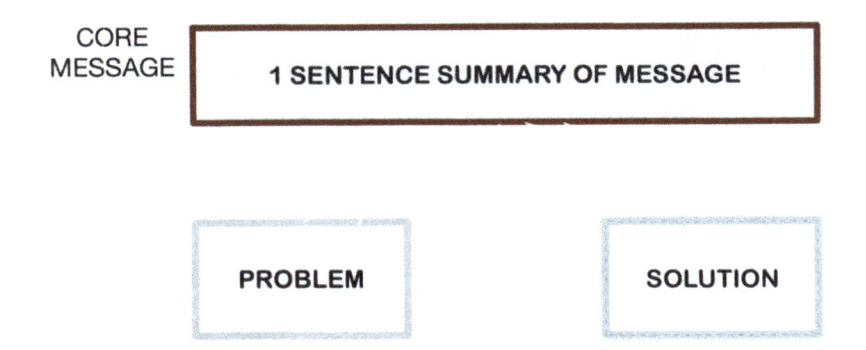

Cause/Effect or Effect/Cause: Considering cause then effect, or vice versa

Core Message: Smoking Causes Lung Cancer

Box 1: Smoking (Cause)   Box 2: Lung Cancer (Effect)

Or

Box 1: Lung Cancer (Effect)   Box 2: Smoking (Cause)

Chronological/Process:

Core Message: It is easy to make a video.

Box 1: Recording (Step 1)   Box 2: Editing (Step 2)

Note: Process organization may be the only organizational strategy which would allow for more than two boxes to be held in short-term memory, as steps of a process are easy to recall and visualize.

Or

Core Message: Abraham Lincoln lived a great life.

Box 1: Early Years   Box 2: Later Years

Compare/Contrast:

Core Message: There are both positive and negative considerations in re-launch.

Box 1: Positives   Box 2: Negatives

Geographical or Spatial:

Core Message: A road trip through France is easy to organize.

Box 1: North   Box 2: South

Order of Importance:

Core Message: All considerations are not equal.

Box 1: Most Important   Box 2: Of Secondary Importance

Narrative:

Core Message: Our business has changed dramatically over the past three years.

Box I: What We Used to Do   Box 2: What We Do Now

Sparklines:

Core Message: Emerging technologies are exciting.

Box I: What Is (Status Quo)   Box 2: What Could Be (Possibility)

Boundary Conditions:

Core Message: Manage your spending when renovating a house.

Box I: Identify Minimum Spend   Box 2: Identify Maximum Spend

(Topical, Problem/Solution, Cause-Effect, Chronological & Spatial organizational strategies: Beebe & Beebe, 2019)

It's a good idea to memorize these organizational options so that you are able to select the most fitting option on the spot, right when you need it.

> **EVERYDAY CONVERSATION PRACTICE:**
> 1. Practice visualizing and using the Message Map when replying to questions. The more you use the structure, the more quickly it will become intuitive.
> 2. Use the Message Map to plan and structure short prepared messages to deliver in meetings, structured conversations, or interviews.
> 3. Practice discerning which organizational strategy is most appropriate for a particular type of topic by implementing the strategies in conversational messaging; with practice the strategies will be easy to recall in impromptu speaking situations.

MESSAGE MAP

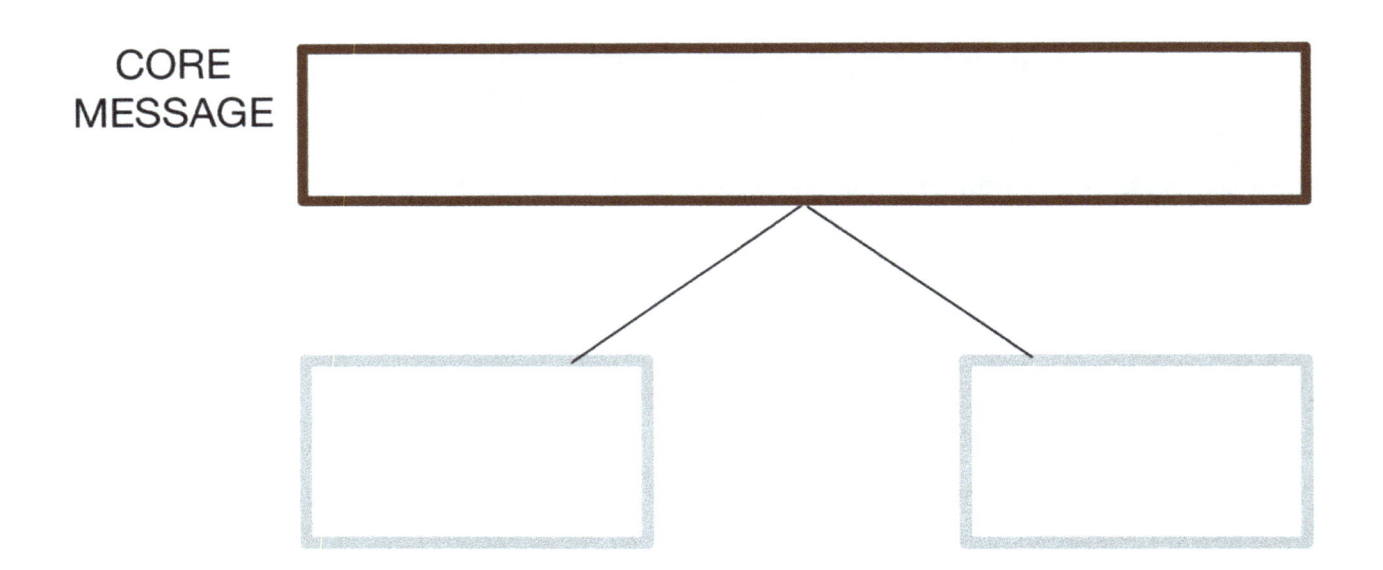

CORE MESSAGE

Inform

Speaking to Inform. Easy, Right?

What could go wrong?

https://www.ted.com/talks/bill_clinton_my_wish_rebuilding_rwanda?utm_campaign=tedspread&utm_medium=referral&utm_source=tedcomshare

Informative speaking is the most common speaking purpose. We deliver information on a daily basis, from explaining process, to giving directions, to elaborating on theory.

While it appears to be an easy task, we need to be mindful to use intentional thinking to design a presentation. Without design, we can end up delivering a glut of incomprehensible information which is boring to listen to and utterly forgettable.

Every message should have a **clear and specific purpose.** When that purpose is unclear to the speaker, it will most certainly be unclear to the audience.

A second important consideration is this: What makes information desirable and palatable is the element of **novelty.** In *Made to Stick*, Chip and Dan Heath iterate *unexpected* as a key quality of data which has the power to stick with our audience. Our innate desire for novelty is inherent in our consumption of information, but often a detail easily forgotten in a speaker's preparation.

We have little interest in hearing what we already know; we are likely to be bored and demotivated by a speaker who delivers data with which we are already familiar. This makes sense at a very basic cognitive level; why waste precious energy and resources processing known facts?

Choosing a Topic

The first step in choosing an informative speech topic is to be certain that the **topic** satisfies one or both of the conditions below:

1. Provides new information
2. Delivers a novel perspective on known information.

This means that *basic health and wellness, how to make a peanut butter and jam sandwich, explaining how to write an essay,* are not great topics for an adult audience. These topics might work for younger listeners who are unfamiliar with the information, but not for most adults.

While this may seem like an obvious point, it is surprising to note how many speakers include reams of uninteresting, redundant content.

Quality not Quantity

It's easy to make the mistake in thinking that it is better to deliver more information rather than less information. While this may be forgivable in written text (still not a good idea), it is not forgivable in public speaking. The primary reason for being cautious with information management is because of the limitation of our **cognitive load**, as discussed in the chapter entitled *Data Overload Is Dangerous. This limitation must be kept in mind during the preparation of a presentation, in order for that presentation to be successful.*

Considerations

When choosing a topic, you should consider:

1. Your own knowledge and experience (**speaker credibility**) with regard to the topic.

    It is much more effective, not to mention much less stressful, to discuss a topic with which you are already familiar. Talk about what you know.

2. The **context** in which you will be speaking.

    Is it a formal event, a lunch and learn talk for executives, a class speech?

    How much time is allotted for the presentation?

    What does the presentation space look like?

    What is the tone of the event?

3. The **audience**.

    Who are the audience members?

    What do they already know about this topic?

    How will they use this information?

When choosing and narrowing a topic for the audience, it is important to consider the *Prospect Awareness Scale.*

The *Prospect* Awareness Scale was developed by Eugene Schwarz and explained in his book *Breakthrough Advertising* (1966). While this scale was first intended for marketing purposes, it applies equally to all prospects or audiences. We are always selling; sometimes we sell products or services, but mostly, we sell ideas.

While the scale is often used in persuasive communication, it has direct application to informative messaging as well. It is essential to identify our specific audience's level of awareness so that we may successfully target their attention and interest.

Prospect Awareness Scale

FULLY AWARE

Fully aware that your idea/product is the best option; repeat "customers."

IDEA/PRODUCT AWARE

Aware that your idea/product is the best choice but needs more data.

SOLUTION AWARE

Aware of the potential solutions; unaware of which solution is best.

PROBLEM AWARE

Senses that there is a problem, but doesn't know where to find a solution.

UNAWARE

No knowledge that a problem or need exists

Imagine that you have been asked to deliver a short presentation to a group of colleagues. You have been assigned to tell them that your company has just acquired new software and to show them how to use it.

If you're like most people, you would likely go in to the meeting and immediately start talking about the new software:

> *Okay everyone, next month we are starting to use Software X. Let's go through how to use it. I have a short demonstration to show you and then I will take questions, if we have time. Step one...*

Here is the problem. As soon as you start talking about Software X, Bob and Joe in the back row look at each other.

Bob: *Software X? Are you kidding? Who has time for this! I use Software A.*

Joe: *Me too! Yeah, I'm good. I don't need new software.*

Then they both proceed to tune out. They are unaware of the problem and therefore mistakenly think that this information is irrelevant to them.

What should you have done differently?

In this case, you should have ensured everyone was on the same page to start. Always begin at your audience's awareness level. If they don't know that software A is going to be phased out in the next month, you need to tell them. Often we assume that our listeners possess information that they do not have.

You: *Here's the problem. Most of you are using Software A. We have discovered that this software no longer meets our growing needs as a company. Therefore we will be replacing this software at the end of the month.* (Now they are problem aware)

But wait...don't just dive in to explaining Software X, because in doing so, you would be jumping ahead to the idea/product aware level and skipping the solution awareness level.

You: *We will now be using Software X... If you start here,* you are skipping a logical step in the audience's thinking process, which is the consideration of alternative options. They might wonder if you could update the current software, purchase a slightly less expensive software, or use an add-on, etc. They mentally need to consider these options before they are told the preferred option.

A good speaker will review these options with them and show why Software X has been chosen over the alternate options.

Always begin at the level above your audience's awareness level. If your audience is unaware, begin by telling them the problem. If the audience is problem aware, begin by discussing possible solutions to the problem. If they are solution aware, (meaning they are aware of all possible options already) explain why your product or idea is the best choice. If they already know the best option, elaborate with details to make them fully aware.

The key to successful speaking is intentional thinking.
Making intelligent and deliberate choices before we speak ensures that we deliver *the best version* of the message we wish to deliver. When it comes to messaging, small changes can make a big difference.

Cognitive science should inform our choices when preparing a presentation.

We need to pay attention to how people actually learn and how they receive information.

The template below is designed with cognitive science principles in mind to ensure that audience attention, comprehension and retention are achieved successfully.

Inform 83

The Five Template Questions for Effective Message Design AKA THE BLUE PENTAGON

THE BLUE PENTAGON
© studiostoks/Shutterstock.com

The blue pentagon is a speaker's best friend. It is both a tool for preparing content and **a** framework **for delivery.**

Preparation

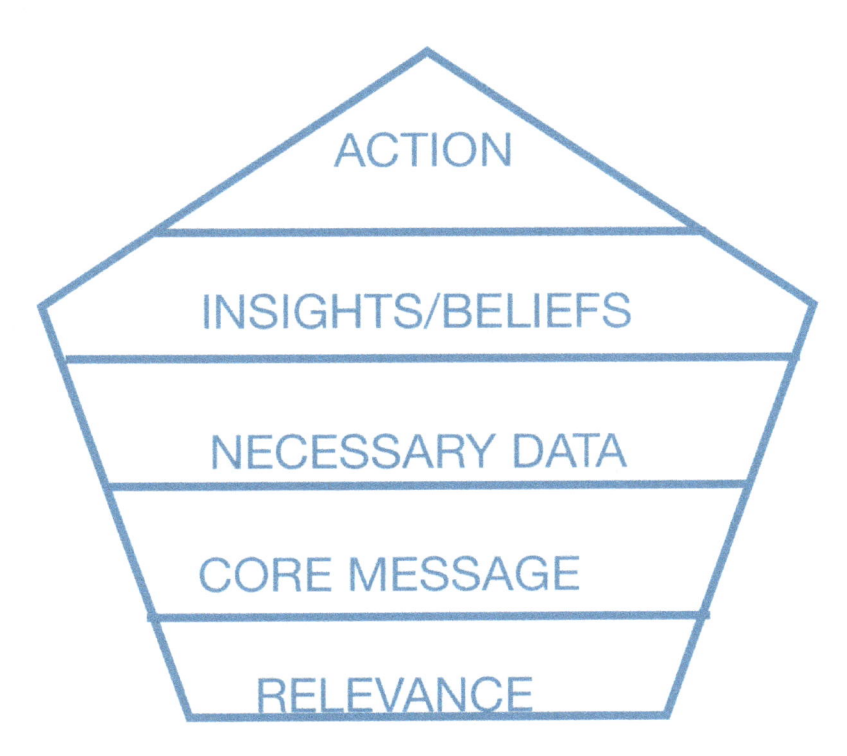

ACTION

INSIGHTS/BELIEFS

NECESSARY DATA

CORE MESSAGE

RELEVANCE

Flip for Delivery

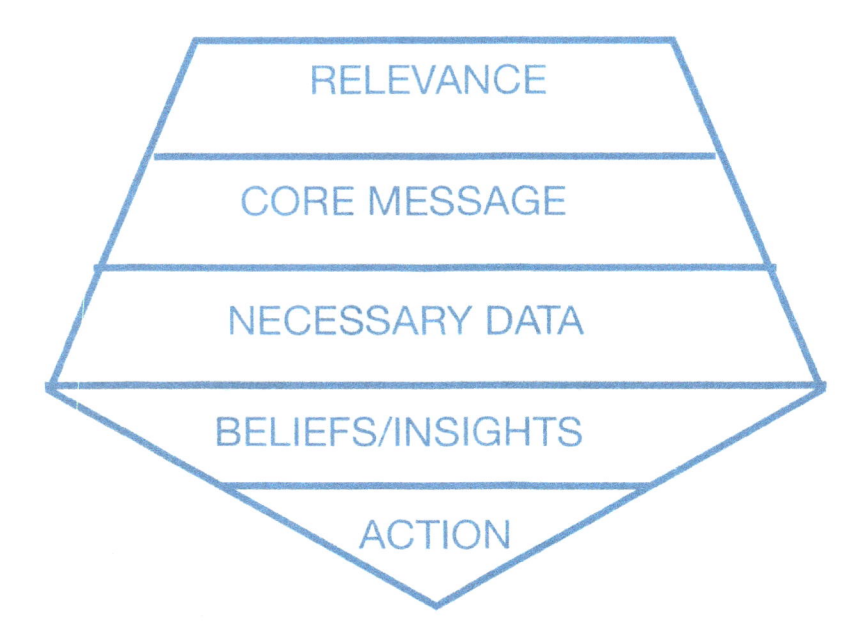

```
        RELEVANCE
       CORE MESSAGE
      NECESSARY DATA
      BELIEFS/INSIGHTS
          ACTION
```

The pentagon may be used to develop any informative message, whether brief or extended.

The blue pentagon consists of five key questions for the speaker to consider.

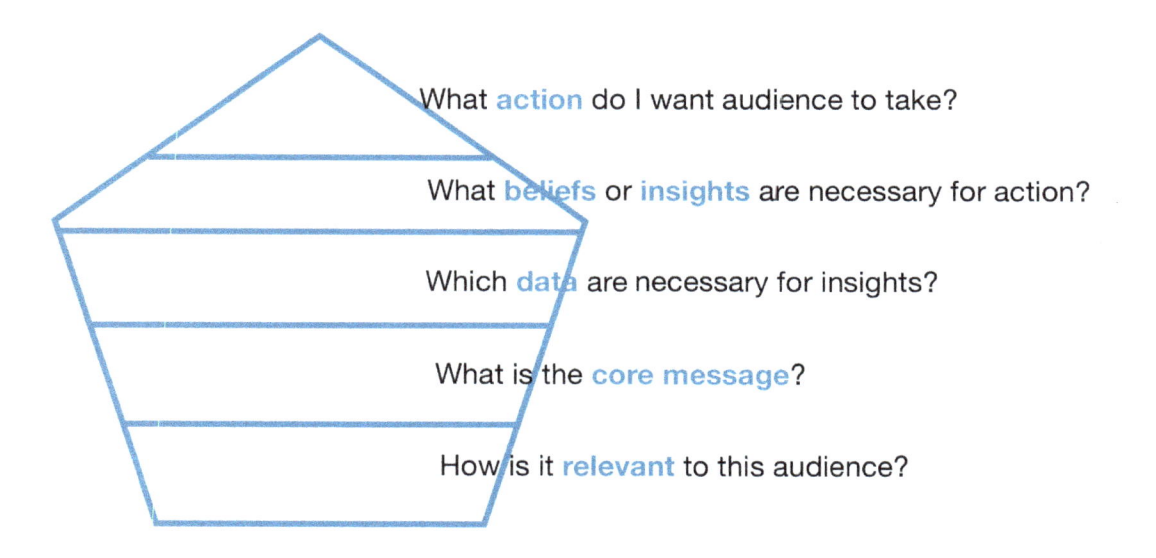

What *action* do I want audience to take?

What *beliefs* or *insights* are necessary for action?

Which *data* are necessary for insights?

What is the *core message*?

How is it *relevant* to this audience?

Let's examine each of these questions. Note that while this may take a little time to learn, once you understand, it is quick to use.

Preparation Stage

Answer the questions from top to bottom.

1. **What *action* do I want the audience to take following my presentation?**

   A speaker should desire an action as the outcome for every message, even if that message is informative and not persuasive. Desiring the audience to take action will ensure that there is a clear practical takeaway for the message. A message without a clear takeaway is a waste of time.

   There is always an action.

   The action may be physical or it may be cognitive.

   There may be a temptation to think that we don't need our audience to take action, but to simply create awareness. For example: *I just want my audience to be aware of this policy.*

   Be careful! This is a step toward failure. Ask yourself, *why would my audience need to be aware of this policy?* Digging more deeply will help you to find the action itself. You might find that you want them to be aware of a policy so that the next time they are in a particular situation that they behave in a different way. *This is the action.* Sometimes we have to do a little digging to find the action, but it always there.

   Without an action in mind, an audience leaves a presentation thinking they have wasted their time, or being painfully unaware of what to do with the information they have received. In order for this purposeful action to be clear to the audience, it needs to be clear to the speaker at the earliest stage of preparation.

   The action should be as specific and concrete as possible.

   Let's say you attend a civic meeting on public policy. Likely there won't be a takeaway at all and the speaker will hope that you understood the discussion. This is not great messaging. If however there is a takeaway at the conclusion of the meeting, it might sound something like this: Please note the policy we discussed tonight.

   Please note the policy? When? How? Why? How will I know if it's been *noted*?

   You walk away doing nothing.

   Instead, if a specific, concrete action is requested, you will have a clear understanding of what you should do.

   In the next few days when your company is submitting the proposal for funding, please remember the reasoning behind the policy we discussed today and why it is so crucial for you to implement these changes within the next two weeks. That is a much clearer directive and is much more likely to see follow-through.

   The action is the foundation of the message because it is the end goal. Start with the end in mind.

2. **What insights or beliefs does my audience need to hold in order to take this action?**

   As humans, our actions are dictated and motivated by our beliefs.

   For example, if you are considering buying a Powerball lottery ticket, there are certain beliefs that you need to hold before you will undertake this action. If you don't hold the beliefs, you won't buy the ticket.

   What do you need to believe to be true before you buy a ticket?

   A. You would need to believe that they are giving away the money.

   B. You would need to believe that you have a fair chance of winning; that it is not a fixed draw.

   C. You would need to believe that your life would be better if you won a ridiculous amount of money.

   Identifying the necessary insights is a crucial step in the process, not only to ensure follow-through on the action requested, but also to ensure content retention by the audience.

   Clearly, audiences do not recall 100 percent of content delivered by a speaker. Estimates range anywhere from 5 to 35 percent for information recall from an oral presentation. They are more likely to recall big picture ideas than small details, especially with the progression of time. It is important to think carefully about these big picture ideas, or insights.

   These insights or beliefs may be truths or corrections of misconceptions. Generally speaking, people will not recall more than five big picture ideas from one message. Aim for between two and five insights. Three is the magic number for the brain, so if possible, aim to have three insights.

   For example:

   Desired Action: Use this new software

   Insights: This software is better than our current software.

         I am capable of using this new software.

         The benefits of switching to a new software outweigh the hassle.

   Once you have identified these insights, jot them down in point form.

3. **Which data is *necessary* for these insights?**

   The next step is to ask yourself what kind of data your audience needs to see in order for them to achieve "**aha moments**" (insights).

   IMPORTANT: The key word in this question is ***necessary***.

   Note that the question is **not** *what do I know about this topic or what do I want to say, etc.*

   At this rather early stage in the process, you are developing a **hierarchy** of data. This will save you copious amounts of wasted time going forward.

To answer this question, look at the insights and make a list of necessary data for each insight.

For example, if I want the audience to buy the lottery ticket, they need to have the insight that they have a chance at winning. To reach that insight, what data would be necessary? They might need to see interviews of real people winning the money.

If I want my audience to use the new software and they need to believe that it is superior to the current software, they might need a side by side comparison of the two programs.

Make two lists:

Necessary List

Wish List

Jot down the data you believe to be necessary. Remember that you are aiming for quality of information and not quantity. Look for *best* data. What is the best data available?

Therefore, the data listed under Necessary should be the **best essential data.**

The advantage of having a **wish list** is that it allows for some wiggle room. Sometimes we are not sure what is necessary; if you're not sure, put it on the wish list. Keep the necessary list as absolutes for now. Having a wish list will allow you to include things that you would like to say, or suggestions made by your boss, etc. and to decide if they truly have a place in your presentation.

Oftentimes once you time the presentation with only data from the necessary list, you realize that you have reached or exceeded your time limit. Right away, you know that nothing on the wish list is going to make the cut.

Another benefit of making a wish list is that you have additional content available should you need it. During a question period following a presentation, we are often asked to give additional examples of something discussed in the speech. Rather than scrambling to think of something on the spot, under pressure, you already have the extra data.

If there is too much data on the necessary list, when you time the speech, it means that you need to re-visit your objective (Question #1) in light of the time limit. You might be trying to accomplish too much in your allotted time.

4. **What is my core message?**

    In a single sentence, determine the point of the message. As mentioned in an earlier chapter, it is important that the core message be summarized in **one sentence** to ensure that it is focused and specific.

    Ideally, the core message should not contain personal pronouns but should be an idea that is accessible to anyone who reads it. Therefore *I think Spain is a great travel destination* is not an ideal core message. You might include personal opinions and anecdotes in the speech itself, but the core message should be more universally applicable: *Spain is a great travel destination*.

    It is worth spending time and effort on the core message. A vague idea or ambiguous vocabulary in this sentence will create problems in the entire message at a later stage.

    Small changes in the idea or the wording will make a difference.

Note the differences in the core messages below.

Our company is getting rid of Software A.

Software X is easy to use.

Software X is superior to Software A.

Only the third example suggests a comparison between the two types of software and therefore gives a much broader picture than the earlier examples.

5. **Why is the problem (issue/topic) relevant to this audience, at this moment in time?** AKA **The Big Who Cares?**

    Relevancy should address a current need. We are less motivated to care about things that apply only to our future selves. If necessary to address future concerns, make sure those concerns are in the near, not distant future.

    When you flip the Blue Pentagon for delivery, relevancy will be the first thing you address.

    It will come before any other content in order to get audience **buy in** so that they will give you their full attention.

    If we know that we are going to learn useful, important information, we choose to pay attention from the beginning. The relevancy element is almost a sales pitch. You need to motivate them to listen and care. Without this step, we risk the success of the message itself. If people don't care to listen, it doesn't matter what you say afterward!

Quick Re-Cap:

Answer the Blue Pentagon questions in the order of **1 through 5**. Then **flip** the Pentagon so the order is **5 through 1**. Now you have a framework for delivery.

The next step of the message design process is to transfer the Pentagon details to an expanded Message Map.

Expanded Message Map

The expanded message map is a *visual outline*.

The visual outline will become your practice notes, then your delivery notes.

Transfer the answers from the Blue Pentagon **to the Expanded Message Map.**

The map is useful because it is concise and it is visual. With the exception of the core message, each idea on the map should be written as a **key word or phrase**, not as a sentence. This will prevent you from reading off the map and ensure that you speak conversationally with key word notes.

Important Note: Any Data box on the map may be broken into further subpoints if necessary.

Each subpoint contains more specific information, or examples than the one above it.

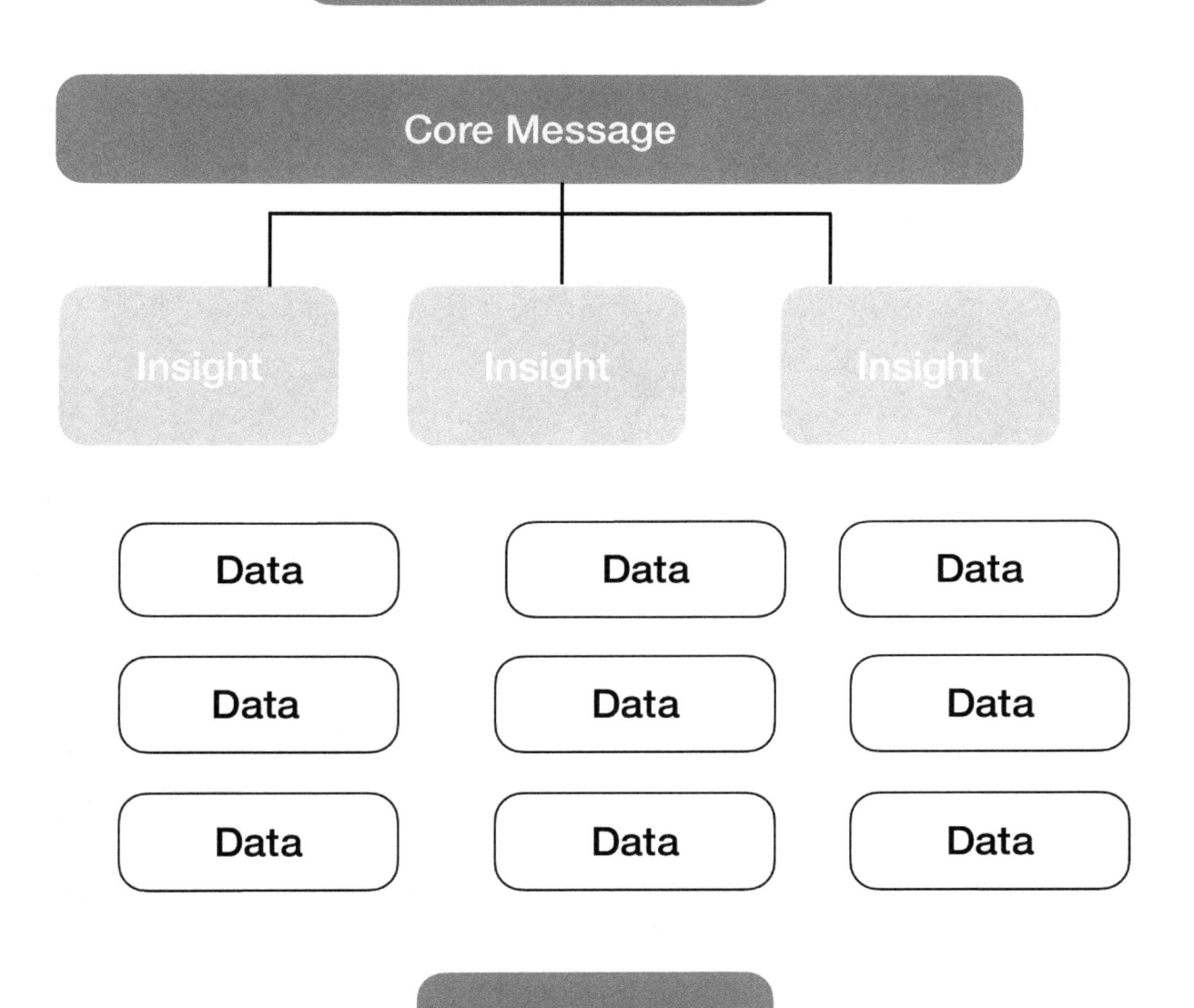

Inform

```
        ┌─────────────────┐
        │    Relevance    │
        └─────────────────┘

┌───────────────────────────────────────┐
│             Core Message              │
└───────────────────────────────────────┘
              │
     ┌────────┼────────┐
┌─────────┐ ┌─────────┐ ┌─────────┐
│ Insight │ │ Insight │ │ Insight │
└─────────┘ └─────────┘ └─────────┘

┌─────────┐ ┌─────────┐ ┌─────────┐
│  Data   │ │  Data   │ │  Data   │
└─────────┘ └─────────┘ └─────────┘
┌─────────┐ ┌─────────┐ ┌─────────┐
│  Data   │ │  Data   │ │  Data   │
└─────────┘ └─────────┘ └─────────┘
┌─────────┐ ┌─────────┐ ┌─────────┐
│  Data   │ │  Data   │ │  Data   │
└─────────┘ └─────────┘ └─────────┘

        ┌─────────────────┐
        │     Action      │
        └─────────────────┘
```

GAB LAB: The Playbook of Public Speaking Prowess Through Everyday Conversation

Could you benefit from saving money every month?

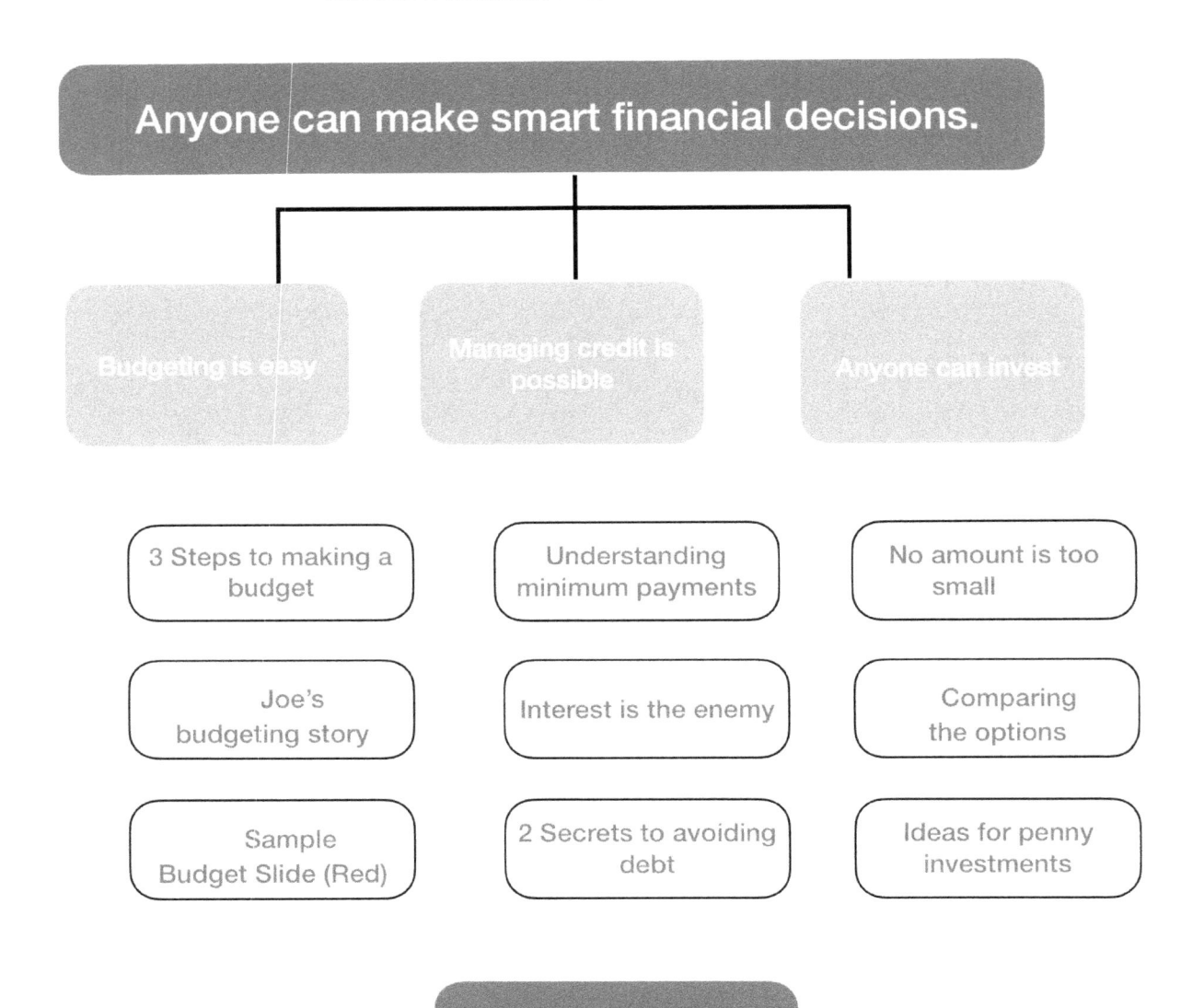

Anyone can make smart financial decisions.

- **Budgeting is easy**
- **Managing credit is possible**
- **Anyone can invest**

Budgeting is easy	Managing credit is possible	Anyone can invest
3 Steps to making a budget	Understanding minimum payments	No amount is too small
Joe's budgeting story	Interest is the enemy	Comparing the options
Sample Budget Slide (Red)	2 Secrets to avoiding debt	Ideas for penny investments

Set a time this month to make a specific plan

The points at the top are more general and become more specific toward the bottom of the map.

Insight
    Data
    Data
        Data
        Data
            Data
            Data
            Data

For example:

Spain is a safe country (Insight)
    Robberies (Data)
    Violent Crime (Data)
        Murder (Data)
        Assault (Data)
            2019 (Data)
            2020 (Data)

While there is no rule on how many subpoints of an idea are allowed, you should never have a single subpoint. The reason for this is a matter of logic. If I break *Dogs* into two categories, I may end up with *Dalmatians* and *Poodles*, but if I only have a single subcategory, *Dalmatians*, then I am not dividing the category of dogs at all. I simply need to re-name the *Dogs* category as *Dalmatians*.

An analogy: If you have a piece of chalk and you break it, you automatically end up with at least two pieces. If you break an idea, you must end up with at least two subpoints.

Note: It is possible to reverse the order of insights and data in delivery. We can deliver the data first in order to point to each insight. If you choose to present the information this way, be sure to make it clear that each set of data is leading up to a point or insight. Choose whichever structure best suits your message.

i.e.
    Data
    Data
    Data
        Insight

The next step is to tweak the map based on the **Six Secrets of Data Design**

Six Secrets of Data Design

Use Primacy:

Place the **strongest** data closest to the **top** of the map.

Studies have indicated that primacy is more effective for long-term memory (Stone 1969; Greene, Prepscius, and Levy 1999; Barkley and Major 2020)

You will arrange data under appropriate insights. The most compelling data should go **first** under each insight. It is true that people recall what they hear last in a presentation and this is why a strong, specific directive is necessary at the end of the speech; here however, we are referring to the placement of data *within* the speech.

For example, if you have three reasons for change, *efficiency*, *economics*, and *ease of use*, the most compelling reason should be delivered first.

Imagine answering a question at a job interview and being cut off before you have finished speaking. You would want to ensure that your most important information had been delivered. Primacy is like information insurance.

This arrangement will allow you to **adapt your message on the spot.**

In order to **shorten** a message, you may the cut the map **horizontally.**

In the example above, *Robberies* is a more important point than *2020* as it is a more *general* idea and therefore more necessary to understand the core message. The data closest to the top is the most important. You would be able to stop speaking after *Robberies* and *Violent Crime*, without adding the additional examples, before moving on to the next insight.

You will be able to eliminate specific data while keeping all of the insights intact.

Conversely, if you were to need to **add** more information, you could add additional examples by adding more specifics at the end of each row of data.

If using many subpoints of data, it is helpful to number them with **Standard Outline numbering:**

I Insight

    A. **Data (Most compelling data: primacy)**

    B. Data

        1. Data (Examples of B)

        2. Data

            a. Data (Examples of 2)

            b. Data

            c. Data

            d. Data

                i) Data (Examples of d)

                ii) Data

When this outline numbering is used on a message map, it allows the speaker to quickly determine their place at a glance.

> Here are the rules:
>
> Roman numerals designate insights
>
> Capital letters designate supporting data of insights
>
> Numbers designate supporting data of supporting data
>
> Small letters designate supporting data of supporting data of supporting data
>
> Small roman numerals designate supporting data of supporting data of supporting data, etc.

It may seem complex here, but it is very simple once you get the hang of it.

This numbering is not mandatory, because the map itself is very visual, but it can be helpful if you have a lot of data.

Manage the Soft: Hard Data Ratio

Hard data, if you recall, take more brain glucose to process than soft data and therefore fatigue the listener at a quicker pace.

We want our audience to stay focused on our message and to avoid taking mental breaks while we are speaking. By ordering our data so that we give the audience those needed breaks, we control their attention.

By using soft data to break up hard data flow, we ease the audience's cognitive load (Chandler, Paul, and Sweller 1991; Pas, Van Gog, and Sweller 2010).

Be sure that you don't have too much hard data (facts, numerical data, visual media) back to back. Aim for a maximum of seven minutes of hard data at once. Then slide in a piece of soft data to allow the audience to breathe and replenish brain glucose. This break need only take thirty seconds before they are ready for another seven minutes of hard data. Using an example, an analogy or a story between hard data is simple and very effective information management.

It has been suggested that the ideal data ratio for an oral presentation is 4:1 soft: hard data.

Use four pieces of soft data for every one piece of hard data. While this may sound impossible for speakers in data heavy disciplines like engineering, remember that all you need is thirty seconds worth of soft data---a joke, a photo, etc. Remember that humans are the same regardless of their job titles. People get overwhelmed with content very quickly. Information management is your responsibility.

Zoom In/Zoom Out

As communicators, we all have tendencies. Some of us tend to be big picture thinkers and spend most of our communication time on big picture ideas, often to the neglect of details.

Others tend to get wrapped up in details and miss big picture concepts.

Big picture thinkers tend to discuss abstract concepts without the necessary examples. Sometimes politicians are guilty of this. We hear about economic policies, fiscal futures, budgetary constraints, but without the examples necessary to clarify, we don't really know what they are saying.

Speakers who are more detail-oriented give lots of examples and nitty-gritty detail, but fail to address why we should care, why these ideas are important, what they mean, etc.

The solution to this problem is to avoid remaining zoomed out on big ideas, or zoomed in on details for too long at any given time. There is no set time for changing our zoom lens; it will depend on the content; however, we may consider three minutes as a general guideline. If you are discussing a big concept, make sure to zoom in to details or examples after three minutes. If you are using details, be sure to give us an overview of the significance after three minutes.

Map the Visuals

Visual media should be integrated into the message map.

As mentioned in an earlier chapter *Beware of the Competition,* the decision to use visuals should be conscious and intentional. If you do decide that you need visuals, plan them into your message map. Visual media is a type of data and therefore may occupy a data box. The keyword in the box may say *Graph 2019 or Video: Mr. Brown, etc.* It is a good idea to identify a visual by placing a red border around the data box so that it will stand out. In this way, when you are speaking using the map and you see a red box, you know that you need to pop up your visual at that particular time. There is no need for PowerPoint slide notes or additional notes. Everything can be indicated on the message map.

Plan Engagement

Remember that good informative speaking does not consist of spoon-feeding the audience information. The more you can engage them both **physically** and **cognitively**, the more successful the outcome (Barkley and Major 2020). The audience should not be passive listeners. Make them do some work. Leave sentences unfinished, ask questions, quiz them, let them see you draw a diagram and wonder to themselves how the finished product will look.

This is easier than you think, yet makes a big difference in their retention.

For example: Instead of telling your audience that there are four reasons that small businesses fail in their first year by simply listing off the four reasons (no engagement) you could instead tell them that there are four reasons and ask the audience to guess what they are. Give a hint by giving the first letter of each answer. We love mystery and we love competition. Use them both.

L

I

P

C

Your audience will guess: Lack of capital? Liquidity problems? Etc.

It doesn't matter whether or not they guess correctly; it matters that they engage with you.

This method works because of the Knowledge Gap phenomenon and it is one of the super-learning principles. As soon as we are aware that there is something we don't know, we want to know it.

Build In Memory Triggers

Figure out when and where your audience will be when taking the desired action. Try to build in a trigger to help them remember the action when the time comes. If you are asking them to do something right away, they will remember your request word for word or verbatim.

For example, *Vote Bob!* is a **verbatim** memory trigger. If the election is two days from your speech, they will remember the slogan. When they see Bob's name on the ballot, the chant *Vote Bob* will come back to them and they can take action.

If, however, the action will be undertaken in the distant future, you need to build in **gist** memory triggers so that when the time comes they will remember the big idea of what they are supposed to do (Simon 2016). If the election is three months away, they might not remember the name of the candidate. It would be better to remind them of the political party for whom you want them to vote. *When you see the green signs, remember to vote for the Green Party.*

Introductions and Conclusions

The most important element in an intro (relevance) and the most important element of a conclusion (the call to action) are already built into the message structure. These are absolutes which should never be omitted.

Generally speaking, an **introduction** should include two elements:

Hook (Relevance)

Overview of Insights

Sometimes we need to establish speaker credibility in an introduction in a very explicit manner *I have been working with this organization for fourteen years*, for example, while other times a moderator may establish that explicit credibility for us.

A **conclusion** should include:

Brief review

A call to action (takeaway)

Sometimes speakers like to add other content to the intro and conclusion, but be mindful of cognitive limitations. If it's not necessary, leave it out.

EVERYDAY CONVERSATION PRACTICE:

1. We deliver information daily in casual conversation. **Identify your own tendencies**. **Practice implementing one strategy** at a time in your conversations to form new habits. For example, when giving directions, be sure begin with an overview and to conclude with a brief review. Be sure zoom in and zoom out. *It's a twenty-minute drive (overview). Take three left turns in a row on Buena Drive, Buena Gate, and Buena Boulevard (details). After the third turn you should see a gas station on your left. (Big picture).*

2. **Start small**. Design a brief message using the **Blue Pentagon** and **Expanded Message Map.** Use these to plan and deliver a simple message at a meeting or in small group setting so that when you have to deliver a longer presentation, the format will be second nature to you.

3. **Start managing your data ratios** in everyday conversation. Avoid giving too much hard data at once. (You know you're doing this when your friend's eyes start to glaze over or he starts looking over your shoulder at the squirrels.)

4. **Consider the Prospect Awareness Scale** the next time you are giving someone information. Are you addressing them at the correct level? Try to identify how much information someone has before you start to speak. This is more effective and less painful for everyone.

Inform 91

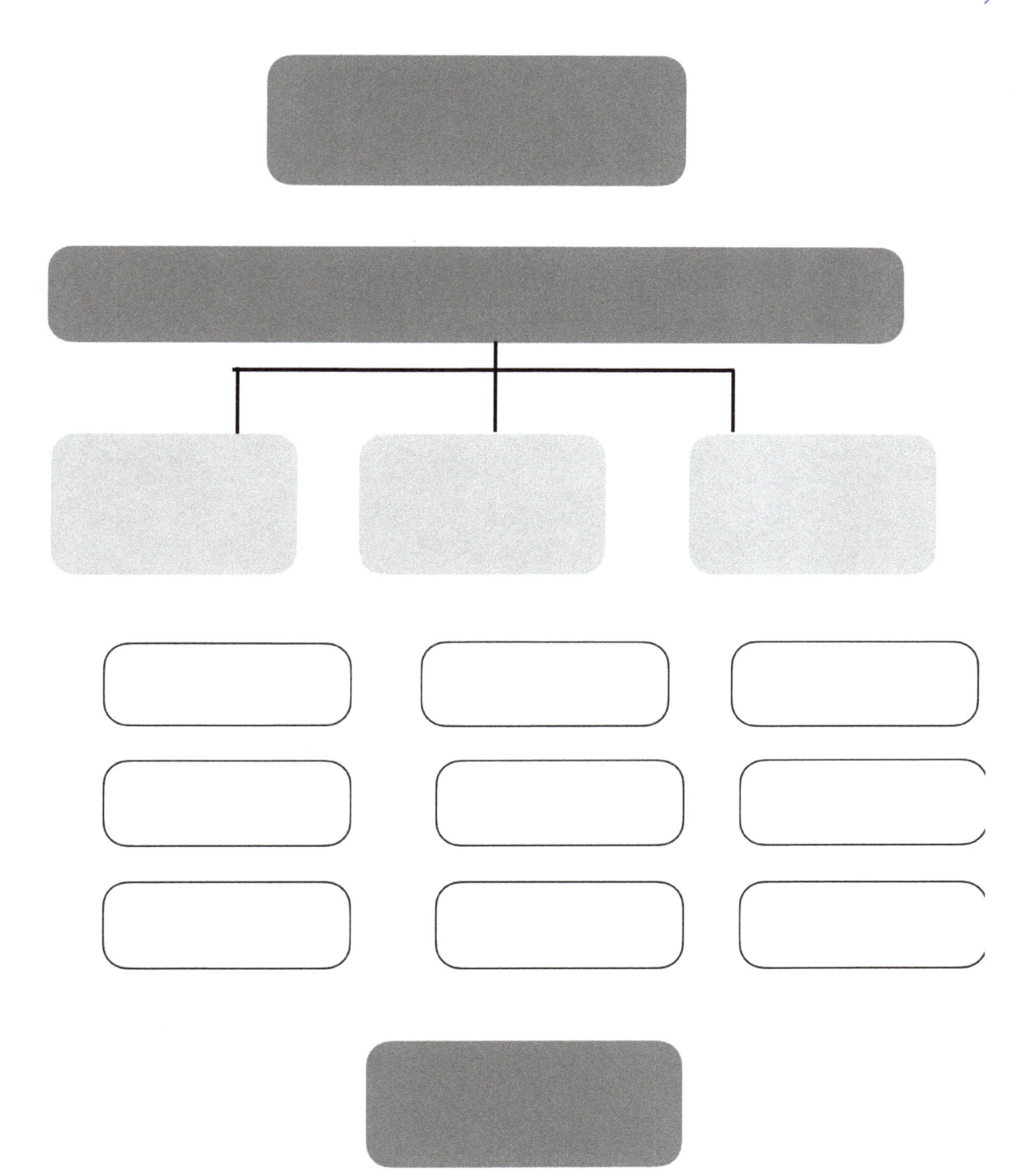

Narrate

"Brown M&Ms"

https://youtu.be/_IxqdAgNJck

© tichr/Shutterstock.com

Life is a story.

(Also a highway, according to Tom)

We think and speak in narratives all day long. Storytelling is the most intuitive form of communication for human beings. We are already storytellers. Storytelling is not something to add to our arsenal, it is something to finesse.

We all love a good story.

Historically, stories and traditions were passed orally from one generation to another; today we are a culture submersed in Netflix, feature films (and hopefully some really good books). Either way, the telling and enjoyment of story is in our blood.

From a public speaking perspective, there are more good reasons to use storytelling or narration.

Why Use Stories

1. **When we tell a story, people listen differently than they listen to other types of data.**

    For example:

    A recent study conducted in April 2020, by Leger and the Association for Canadian Studies, concluded that 60 percent of Canadians are in support of a mandatory Covid-19 vaccine, while 40 percent oppose the idea.

    Think about how you receive that information when you hear it. You might think that 60 percent is a low number, considering that everyone you know personally supports the idea of a mandated vaccine. You may then be skeptical of whether or not the statistic is accurate. You might wonder about the source of the study. Have you ever heard of this particular association?

    Your brain is often (and ideally) in analytical mode when you hear hard data. You process it rationally, analytically and with skepticism.

    Now consider this:

When I was driving to work this morning, I saw a huge accident at the intersection of Highway 1 and Rosemont Boulevard. There was a blue truck that had turned left in front of a semi.....

Think about how you receive this kind of information, an anecdotal story. Do you question that the accident really took place at the intersection of Highway 1 and Rosemont Boulevard? Do you think to yourself "Are you sure it was *Rosemont Blvd*?" Probably not. You likely accept the story at face value. Why? Because your critical thinking system was not activated. You heard and processed the story in System 1, or your intuitive, emotional thinking system.

System 1 is our default processing system because it requires less mental and physical energy. We prefer to process in System 1 because it is easier for us. It is very unlikely, except in particular circumstances then, for an audience to process a story in System 2.

Because listeners process stories (and all soft data) with their noncritical processing system, they are much more open and vulnerable to accepting this information without thinking about it critically. This presents an opportunity for the speaker.

Listeners do not expect to be influenced by narratives and therefore their guard is down (Cin et al. 2004).

Due to the fact that listeners have their critical editor turned *off* while listening to stories, a speaker may incorporate a point which would be otherwise received critically through a different form. Listeners may buy into an idea presented through story, that they might otherwise consider rejecting when presented as data. A speaker, therefore, can use this to her advantage, as long as it is done ethically.

2. **Stories help forge connections on a biological level.**

    Neuroeconomic studies show that stories encourage the production of oxytocin, which motivates empathy and cooperation (Zak 2005).

    When we tell stories to a listener, our brains actually synchronize. If the speaker shows activity in his insula, the listener will mirror the same activity in his insula. Speaker and listener forge a mysterious connection through story.

    Another interesting fact is that when a listener hears a story, various parts of the brain are activated. Unlike listening to a series of facts, where the language part of the brain alone is activated, stories activate many brain areas, which allow for a simulated experience of the story. When we hear about someone brewing a dark roast Italian espresso, we can almost taste it ourselves. This phenomenon is called **neural coupling.**

3. **Stories have significant power to engage and influence.**

    Studies show consistent findings which indicate that stories have significant power to influence ideas.

    Here are just a few examples:

    The highest viewer-ranked TED talks rely primarily on narrative.

When listening to a story, an audience does so actively, constructing the story in his own mind (Oatley 2013). This active participation increases engagement. Engagement increases recall, which in turn increases the potential for influence.

Narratives emerged as the most effective choice when the goal is to target and change audience attitudes (Reinhart et al. 2007).

In the field of science communication, narratives have been shown to be more effective than logical-scientific format, in changing negative perceptions (Yang and Hobbs 2020). While people may seek out hard data to supplement and confirm a theory, the power of narrative as a primary motivator is undeniable.

How to Tell a Great Story, Visualized (TED Blog)

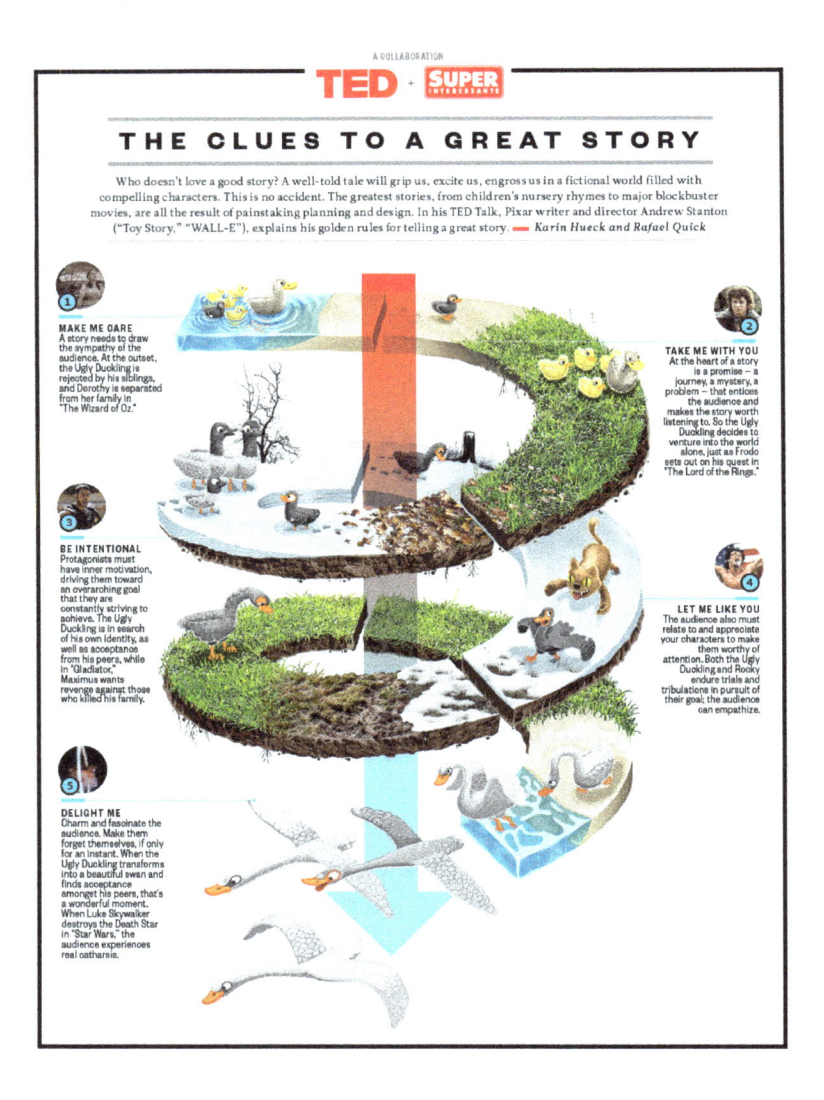

Adapted from screenwriters, filmmakers, and storytelling gurus, here are seven principles of effective storytelling:

Seven Principles of Effective Storytelling

1. **Parachute In**

   Parachuting in has two elements.

   First, it means avoiding unnecessary preamble at the beginning of a story.

   (Schramm, Seven Secrets to Storytelling Success, *From Cafe Scientifique* Youtube, 2014)

   Think of when you buy a ticket to hear a speaker. Before the speaker begins, a random guy comes on stage and welcomes you to the event, tells you where to find the washrooms, thanks a few sponsors, etc.

   How much attention do you pay to this guy? If you're like most people, probably not much. We hear his voice in the background while we check our phones one last time, say something to our friend, get comfortable in our seat, etc. We know this stuff isn't important, but when the speaker comes on stage, we listen differently.

   The reality is that *we ourselves* often give the unnecessary preamble to the audience. When we say *Hi everyone, I'm just going to tell you this story about this great thing that happened to me with my friends last summer and .....* the audience subconsciously recognizes this as unnecessary information and they tune out. The problem is that it is harder to get them to tune back in once they have tuned out, so we don't want to lose them in the first place. That's number one.

   The second element is **jumping in with a teaser**.

   Your first sentence in a story should grab attention in such a way that it makes the audience want to know more. If this fails to happen, we can easily tune out.

   Imagine that you like crime shows and that at 9:00 p.m. there are two crime shows on TV.

   You are trying to decide which one to watch, so you flip to the first channel. You see a few cops sitting around an "incident room" and they are chatting about one of the cops' ex-wives. Then you flip to the second channel. There you see some officers with flashlights crunching through leaves in the pitch dark. The music in the background makes you apprehensive. Suddenly the flashlight illuminates a bone on the ground. Which show are you going to watch?

   Probably the second. Why? You're going to watch it because it has grabbed your attention and left you curious to find out more information. Is it a human bone? How long has it been there? How will they figure it out? Teasers motivate us to keep paying attention.

   Note the difference below in the two versions of the same story.

Version 1:

My Uncle Rob was born in Oregon in 1947. Rob grew up on a farm with his three siblings. He married his high school sweetheart Nellie after graduating from Oregon State with a degree in finance. Rob and Nellie had six children: Joseph, Lily, blah blah blah...(Boring, right?)

Version 2:

I never thought that my uncle Rob would end up in jail.

Let me back up. Rob was born in Oregon in 1947........

The only difference is that single sentence teaser at the beginning, but now, you are much more motivated to pay attention.

2. **Choose Details Wisely**

Choose to include only details which serve the story and keep it moving. Do we need to know that it was a dark and stormy night? Maybe. If the time of day and the weather add to the mood you want to create for the audience, then it does matter. If it is irrelevant detail, then leave it out.

There can be a fine line between including not enough detail and giving too much detail. As communicators, we all have habits and tendencies. Many people tend to give too many details and add unrelated tangents. These tangents can take the audience out of the story. You lose the audience and the magic when you are too verbose.

Not enough detail doesn't allow the audience to engage their senses fully and to participate in the story's journey.

3. **Show Not Tell**

You may recognize this as a principle of good writing. It is also a principle of good speaking.

Instead of telling people something, allow them to discover it on their own by your use of example and detail (*The Screenwriter's Bible*, David Trottier, 1994).

Here is the difference between showing and telling:

Telling:

Anthropology 2075 is a terrible course. It's very difficult and the professor has unrealistic expectations not to mention poor communication skills.

Showing:

I took this course called Anthro 2075. The first day of class the professor assigned us 200 pages of reading. The following day he gave us a pop quiz on the first 300 pages of the book. When a student spoke up and mentioned that we had only been assigned 200 and not 300 pages, he slammed his hand on the desk and told us that we had better start paying attention if we wanted to pass the course. Then we took a quiz on the first 300 pages.

When we tell people something, we force a conclusion upon them and they do not share in the experience; it remains unique to the speaker. When we show, we invite listeners in to share the experience, by allowing them to engage intellectually and emotionally and to reach their own conclusion. (Note that in the showing version you weren't told that it was a terrible course, but you likely reached that conclusion yourself.)

4. **Use Concrete Language**

    Concrete language enables visualization of images. You can visualize a blue teapot; you can visualize a veranda overlooking the Algarve. You cannot visualize core competency, synergy and standard deviation (but you might feel a yawn coming on).

    As discussed in an earlier chapter, the brain recalls images, not concepts. For this reason, we need to speak in concrete language so that our audience can visualize what we mean and then remember it. Ask yourself, can I *picture* this idea? If not, find another way to say it.

    There are times, however, when we can't avoid an abstract word. In that case, make sure you follow the abstraction immediately with a concrete example.

5. **Avoid Implicatures**

    Implicatures are words that do have purpose in the English language, but when used unnecessarily can weaken a message.

    Here is an inconclusive list:

    Just

    Sort of

    Kind of

    Maybe

    You know

    Like

    I don't know

    Sorry

    Really

    I think

    I believe

    I feel

    So

    Etc.

    It is ok to use any of these words in your speech when they have a purpose, but be careful; it's easy to use them as filler words.

For example:

I kind of think, you know, that this rug is, you know, like a bit dirty, maybe. Sorry.

Translation: *This rug is dirty.*

If you need to say the rug is dirty, say the rug is dirty. Avoid using words that add nothing to the meaning of the sentence.

If, however, you don't want to offend your friend, because the rug is *his* rug, you might choose to use implicatures because they soften the message.

When you are calling across a large dinner table to someone on the other side

Sorry, if you wouldn't mind just passing the butter..

does sound a lot more civil than

Pass the butter please.

In summary, avoid implicatures, unless you need to soften a message.

6. **Trigger an Emotional Response**

   Part of a story's impact comes from its power to provoke an emotional response in the audience. Don't leave this to chance and hope that something fires somewhere. Be intentional in choosing what emotion you want to provoke in your listeners and then make it happen with what you choose to show.

7. **Deliver a Lesson or Takeaway**

   One of the reasons we like the narrative form is because we can recognize or imagine ourselves in the context of the story. We not only enjoy a story for entertainment value, but we always hope to glean a little nugget of wisdom. *If MY car ever goes in the river I'll remember not to open the windows at the wrong time.*

   Again, don't leave this to chance. Decide what you hope to give the audience as a lesson or takeaway and make it explicit. This can work with any story, but sometimes you have to look a little harder than with others. In a story about your distant cousin Rosa, we might not be able to relate to your family's experience, but we could all learn, for example, to appreciate an important person whom we don't see very often.

   You are unique and you have unique stories to tell. Every story doesn't have to be about how you saved the world on a Wednesday; every story doesn't need to be earth-shattering, dramatic and life-changing; it only needs to be true. Focus on the small things.

Build a Story Repertoire aka The Story Briefcase

It's a good idea to think about your own personal and professional experiences so that you can build a repertoire of stories to share when the moment is right. (Shawn Callahan: *Putting Stories to Work*)

Practice the stories so that you can articulate them fluently when an occasion presents itself: in job interviews, at networking events and in awkward conversations.

Here are some story prompts to get you thinking. Jot down an idea for each prompt.

A time when you:

*Changed your mind

*Learned something about yourself

*Admired someone

*Accomplished something significant

*Failed miserably

*Surprised yourself

*Faced a dilemma

*Succeeded as part of a team

*Lost/gained faith in something

*Relied on yourself

*Offered good advice

*Threw a great/terrible party

*Felt betrayed

*Were embarrassed

*Rejected a gift

*Had a fantastic idea

*Demonstrated leadership

*Were misunderstood

*Discovered your identity

How to Prepare a Story

1. Storyboard your ideas using sticky notes. Use one sticky note per story event.
2. Talk through the story aloud, using the sticky notes as prompts.
3. Tweak details.
4. Vary rate, volume, pitch and tone for expressive delivery.
5. Time
6. Rehearse

GAB LAB: The Playbook of Public Speaking Prowess Through Everyday Conversation

RUN TO HOUSE Moby Porcelain / Bostones — our only weapon	ENTER HOUSE	> HOLD ON ENVELOPE LONGER SHE'S NOT THERE (EMPTY CHAIR)
HEARS THE CAR > bump up car sfx VROOM VROOM	RUNS OUTSIDE (SEES CAR DRIVING AWAY)	JUMPS OFF DECK

Narrate 109

Everyday Conversation Exercise:

1. Finesse your stories as you relate them in everyday conversations. Trying incorporating one technique or principle at a time. Practice makes good habits.
2. Try telling the same story to a few different people in daily conversation. See how the story details change according to whom you are speaking. A subtle shift will happen automatically but make intentional choices to include (or avoid) specific details when speaking to particular individuals. Targeting your audience will strengthen connections.

Persuade

Let's begin with a story. This is a true story which had massive impact on a large number of people and is a brilliant example of successful persuasion in action.

It is relayed in the book *Power of Moments,* by Chip and Dan Heath and is best told in their own words. (Trip over the Truth: Part 1)

https://bit.ly/SocraticD

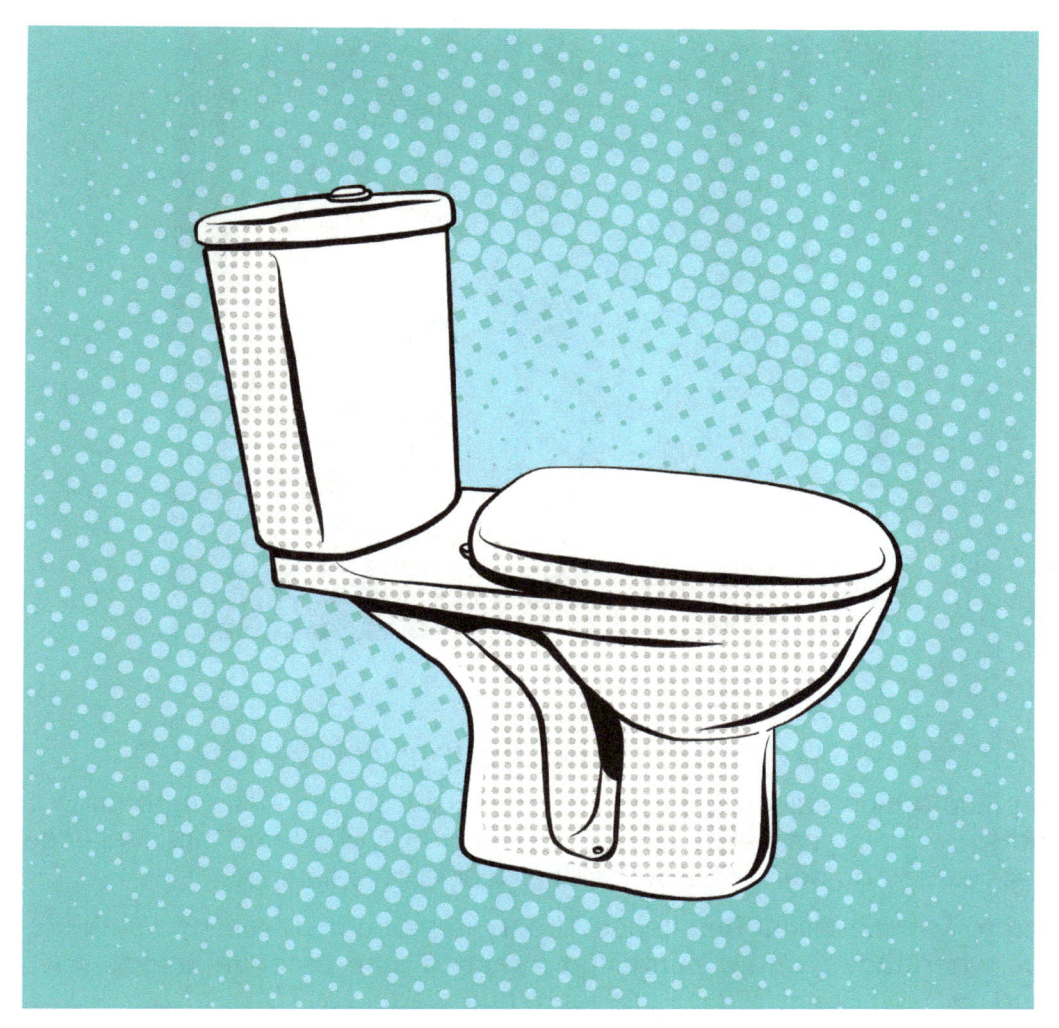

© studiostoks/Shutterstock.com

Persuasion does not happen when an audience decides to accept your idea. Persuasion happens when an audience *discovers* your idea for *themselves*.

Is there a difference? Absolutely. And that difference makes ALL the difference. Persuasion often gets a bad rap. True persuasion is neither coercion nor manipulation.

© yellowline/Shutterstock.com

*The act of persuasion must respect the **autonomy** of the human person.*

Humans place a high value on autonomy. Edward Deci identifies autonomy as one of three innate psychological needs (Deci and Ryan 1987). Anything that challenges autonomy (or appears to do so) will be met with a degree of resistance.

According to Psychological Reactance Theory, a person will respond with a degree of reactance when faced with a perceived threat to their personal freedom (Sharon S. Brehm and Jack W. Brehm1981; Rosenberg and Siegel 2017).

A study by Reich and Robertson (1979) showed that subjects were most resistant to messages with explicit commands. Other studies including one by Dillard and Shen (2005 etc) confirm the negative impact of assertive language and commands, pointing to the assertion that they have a boomerang effect, wherein the recipient is more entrenched in his own position.

Informative versus Persuasive Speaking: The Most Important Difference

Informative and persuasive speaking differ in their basic **structure**.

In an informative message, the speaker should state a clear core message and back it up with evidence. A persuasive speaker should avoid this informative structure at all costs.

Let's use an example to demonstrate why this is so important.

Example:

Bob is a speaker who strongly believes that teachers across America should have guns in their classrooms.

Clearly, this is a controversial topic. People have pre-existing opinions on many controversial topics; some are strong opinions while others are vague uninformed ideas.

For this example, let's imagine that half the audience agrees with Bob's position and the other half disagree with his position. (It is possible that some listeners do not have a position, though most are likely to lean toward one position or another when it comes to considering the topic.)

Bob: *Teachers need guns to protect students in every classroom in America!*

This is the first sentence of Bob's speech and he has already set himself up for failure. He is using what is termed *conclusion explicitness*. Let's examine why conclusion explicitness is problematic.

Imagine that you are part of the audience who *agrees* with Bob. What goes on inside your head when Bob makes this statement? Probably something to this effect:

I totally agree! Right, I already believe this to be true. I'm with you Bob!

While your initial response may be a positive one, because of your agreement with the speaker, now, you have no motivation to pay attention. You may be briefly curious to see what he has to say, but because you have to use brain glucose and energy resources to pay attention, subconsciously you will choose not to waste your energy, because there is no perceived benefit.

Therefore, *half* of the audience is not paying attention.

Now, imagine that instead, you are part of the half that *disagrees* with Bob. What do you do mentally, when someone states something with which you disagree? Studies show (see *resistance* below) that you will make one of two choices: choose to tune out immediately or begin to review your own counterarguments while Bob is speaking.

You might even have a stronger negative reaction: *Oh, one of those people. Here we go. I think this is a terrible idea. I can't wait to challenge him once he stops talking.*

But are you listening attentively to Bob's well-prepared arguments?

No.

Therefore, the *other half* of the class is not paying attention.

So, who IS paying attention to Bob?

No one.

It's impossible to change minds when no one is paying attention.

© Lemon Workshop Design/Shutterstock.com

Question Framing

Framing a controversial topic as a **nonleading question** is more effective than conclusion explicitness in eliciting positive persuasive responses (Brehm and Brehm 1981; Petty & Cacioppo, 1979; 1986; O'Keefe, 1997; Cruz, 1998; Hovland and Mandell 1952).

This is true for both lengthy messages and short appeals.

Instead of using an explicit statement at the beginning of a persuasive argument, use a **nonleading question, or a question which does not give away your position.**

In the example above, the question might be: *Should Teachers in America Have Guns in Classrooms* or *Should Guns in Classrooms Be Mandated for Teachers?*

When a question is framed this way, audience engagement rises significantly. The audience becomes part of an active exploration process. They are curious and willing to pay attention as the argument unfolds before their eyes. They are active rather than passive participants. This makes a big difference on many levels: They don't tune out, they are cognitively engaged in examining and interpreting data, they are satisfying a human need to discover what they don't know (knowledge gap) and are likely to engage in System 2 or critical thinking because they have a job to do (solving a problem).

(Note: The only case in which conclusion *explicitness* has been shown to be preferable to nonexplicitness is in direct marketing appeals. In other words, if you are trying to sell life insurance to a neighbor, make your intention clear right from the beginning. Don't invite him to coffee and reveal that information once he arrives. No one appreciates deceptive tactics.)

Once you have led with a nonleading question, the process of persuasion is very simple. You are going to provide boundaries in which your audience can explore the data. You will gradually lead them through the data on both sides of the argument. By choosing best data and arranging with careful thought, you are leading the audience to discover your predetermined conclusion.

Social Judgment Theory and the Latitude of Noncommitment

A listener's most accepted view on an issue is defined as his *anchor*, and will determine how attitudes inherent in the speaker's message will be received.

Social Judgment Theory (Sherif and Hovland 1961; Carolyn W. Sherif, Muzafer Sherif, and Nebergall 1965, 1981) suggests that it is best to choose a question or perspective within the audience's *Latitude of Noncommitment*.

It is not wise to choose either an idea with which they already agree (Latitude of Acceptance) nor an idea with which they completely disagree (Latitude of Rejection) as it is difficult to engage people in either latitude, based on the fact that audiences will perceive a message similar to their own viewpoint as *closer* to their viewpoint than it actually is and a message in their latitude of rejection as *further* from their own viewpoint than reality suggests.

A Latitude of Noncommitment lies *between* their latitudes of Acceptance and Rejection. It is a perspective on which the audience does not have a position, or may be a new angle or perspective which they have not considered. As discussed earlier, novelty makes people pay attention and in this case, it prevents pre-existing opinions from getting in the way.

Example:

First Nonleading Question:

What should be done with murderers?

Latitude of Rejection: The death penalty (too harsh)

Latitude of Rejection: No punishment (too lenient)

Note that the latitudes of rejection are on *both* sides of the spectrum.

Latitude of Acceptance: Jail time

Latitude of Noncommitment: Jail without parole

This latitude of NC lies *between* jail and the death penalty (on the more punitive side)

Latitude of Noncommitment: Mandatory counseling, community service, and fines

This latitude of NC lies *between* jail and no punishment (on the less punitive side)

Because these in-between positions are less commonly discussed, people are less likely to have strong pre-existing opinions.

When you get someone to agree with an idea which was once in their Latitude of Noncommitment, you have now moved their anchor position and widened their Latitude of Acceptance.

From there, you can, if you wish, gradually move toward their Latitude of Rejection by asking them to consider something within their new Latitude of Noncommitment.

Socratic Dialogue

The Socratic Method is a form of argumentation that is based on questioning. Socrates taught his followers not through explicit statements (informative structure) but by asking sequential questions which would provoke critical thinking and reasoning skills in his listeners, leading them to discover truths through this guided process. This process respects the autonomy of the listener and provokes active engagement.

In its purest form, the Socratic Method takes place when a questioner directs pointed questions to a specific listener, addressing them by name and expects a direct response in return.

In a public speaking environment, this method will take the form of Socratic dialogue.

In Socratic dialogue, the questioner, or speaker, will guide the audience collectively (vs. individually) through a series of predetermined questions to allow them to consider data and to reach their own conclusion.

Persuasion therefore, has its own message map to facilitate planning of a question-framed argument.

The way we approach a persuasive topic will determine the finished product.

If you predecide a conclusion and then search for data to back up your position, it is easy to data-mine information, in other words, to choose only data which supports your position. This approach is problematic because it puts blinders on the speaker from the outset. If you don't see the opposing position in a fair light, you cannot give it fair consideration.

Therefore, although you may have an existing viewpoint on a topic, approach it from the beginning as if you do not.

1. Find a question which interests you and which can be made relevant to your audience.
2. Do preliminary research on the topic, examining arguments on both sides.
3. Determine your audience's level of awareness as determined by the *Prospect Awareness Scale* in the chapter *Inform*.
4. Find your audience's Latitude of Noncommitment.
5. Discover the more compelling position.
6. Use the **Fire Pentagon**
7. Transfer to **Persuasive Message Map**

Boundary Questions

While in informative speaking we use insights, in persuasive speaking these are replaced by secondary or **boundary questions.**

Secondary questions are questions which need to be answered in order to eventually answer the primary question. They also set the boundaries for the argument. The goal is to allow the audience to explore freely, exerting their autonomy, but within constrained boundaries set by the speaker.

For example, if the primary question is: *Should We Support Harm Reduction Programs,* what questions need to be answered in order to finally answer this question?

Depending on your audience's awareness level, the boundary questions may look quite different. In a case where your audience is quite *familiar* with the topic, we may want to ask: Is harm reduction the best option? How will we know if harm reduction is working? Does it provide the best long-term outcome?

If the audience is *unfamiliar* with the topic, the secondary questions might be: Do we have a moral obligation to prevent harm? Does harm reduction actually prevent harm? Is it the best choice?

A number of different boundary questions may be chosen; be sure that the ones you choose are the most effective options to reach your persuasive objective. Make sure that the boundaries you set are going to give your audience enough scope and content for exploration while still controlling the flow of the data.

Best Data

Honest intellectual enquiry consists of examining an idea from varied perspectives. We should always start with a non-leading question, but sometimes we think we already know the answer to the question, before we begin investigating. Sometimes this cannot be avoided, however, be careful. Remember that scientific enquiry consists NOT of proving a hypothesis but by attempting to disprove the null hypothesis. In other words, attempt to disprove what you believe to be true or accurate. If you cannot do so, your hypothesis may be valid. In the scientific method, the data would be subject to a rigorous statistical analysis. While we may not always have the inclination to investigate our topics to this degree, we should respect this process as a guideline to determine whether our conclusions are reasonable.

Choose and present the **best data on both sides of the argument**. The data should be arranged in a logical framework which will allow the audience to understand the story told by the data.

After presenting a single piece of data (on both sides) answer the question: **What does this mean?** This will allow you to draw out implications of the data, which pieced together in a logical framework, will lead your audience to draw a logical conclusion.

This is called data interpretation. This is *not* the same as editorializing the data. Data interpretation asks the question *what does it mean*?

For example: "Vinyl Flooring X has a wear layer of 10 mil (data) while Vinyl Flooring Y has a wear layer of 20 mil" (data).

Ok, so what? We know that the wear layer is greater in Vinyl Flooring Y but *What does this data mean? (Interpretation)* "This means that with Vinyl Flooring Y, your top layer print design will last years longer than with the same flooring with a 10 mil wear layer." Data interpretation helps the audience to *unpack* or understand the *implications* of the data. The implications are not always self-evident.

"*This is a dumb argument*" or "*You can see how this proves my point*" is editorializing the data and should be avoided.

Instead, present the data and let it speak for itself. For example: *Those who are against this position will point you to this study which says.... and The other side would argue that...etc.*

Avoid showing your hand. The audience should not be tipped to your position until at least 75% of the way through the presentation. This can be a challenging task, but it has been shown to be a worthwhile one. The framework of this data/data interpretation can take many forms, but should lead the listener through a linear path to discover a conclusion. For example, *If A, then B, if B, then C, therefore if A then C.*

Lead them to the path with your data and lead them along the path with your data interpretations.

Choose a logical reasoning framework for your data. This framework may be used in one of two places, or both, as you present data on both sides, or as a summary of the best data supporting your position, toward the end of the message.

Causal, Inductive, Deductive, Abductive Reasoning (Framework)

Here are some quick tutorials in logical reasoning: Causal Reasoning: https://www.researchgate.net/publication/229706112_Causal_Reasoning_Psychology_of

Inductive, Deductive and Abductive Reasoning: http://www.butte.edu/departments/cas/tipsheets/thinking/reasoning.html

Creating an Affective Experience

While logical reasoning is essential, it is neither the starting point nor the motivating force behind change. Remember the elephant? In *Switch* by Chip & Dan Heath, the elephant represents System 1 which is the emotional, intuitive driver of human behavior. The rider is not the boss; the elephant is the boss. Logical reasoning devoid of emotional appeal is fruitless.

Emotion is the motivational driver behind our rational choices. It is especially important to recognize the role of emotion in persuasive appeals. We cannot argue devoid of emotion because our listeners are human beings, not robots. Emotional appeals should be used to motivate the audience to care and to be interested in actively engaging with the hard data which will follow in order to make a balanced decision.

In fact, every good persuasive appeal begins with an **experience** which will provoke the audience to an **emotional response**. This emotional response may be positive or negative, but it is the fire behind the momentum of persuasive argumentation.

Therefore, create a visceral experience for the audience, an experience which will provoke an emotional response. This experience will be your hook at the beginning of the speech. Telling your audience that 2 L of water is wasted with every toilet flush does not provide a visceral experience. Pouring 2 L of water on the floor in front of them provides a visceral experience. Be creative.

Fire Pentagon

Preparation

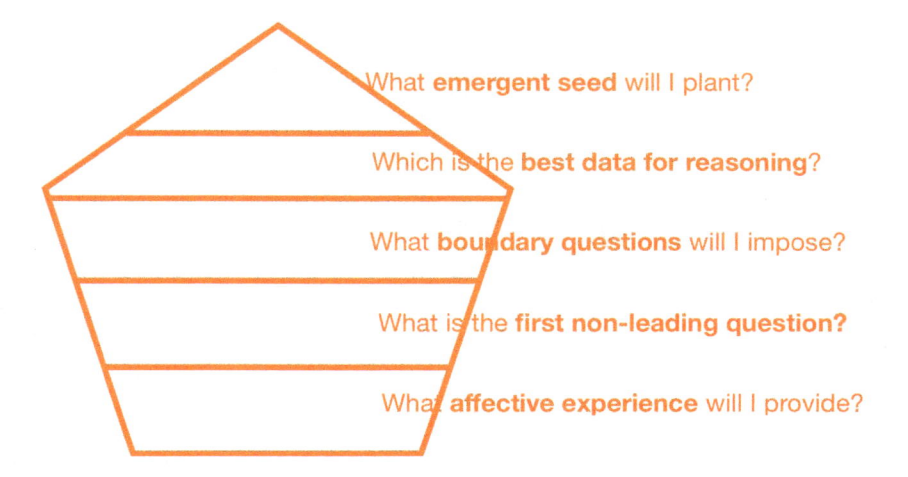

- What **emergent seed** will I plant?
- Which is the **best data for reasoning**?
- What **boundary questions** will I impose?
- What is the **first non-leading question?**
- What **affective experience** will I provide?

Delivery

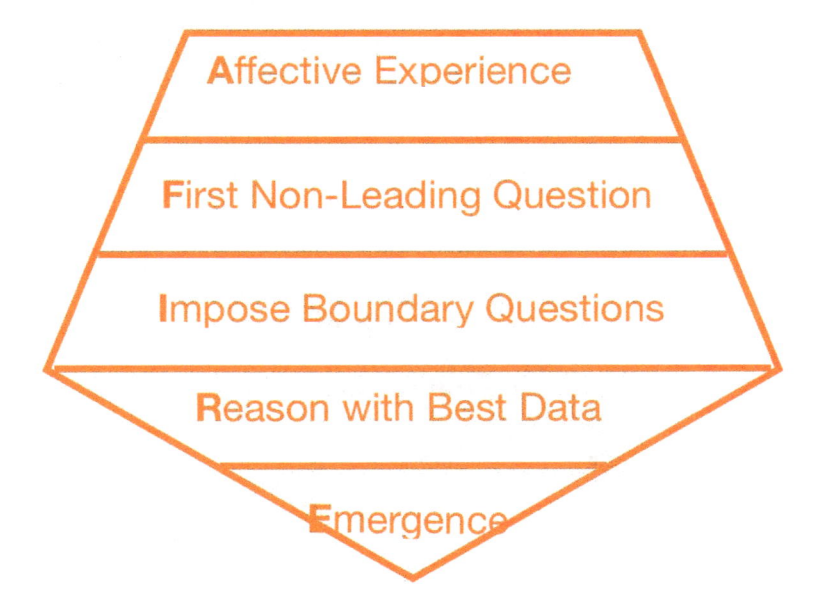

- **A**ffective Experience
- **F**irst Non-Leading Question
- **I**mpose Boundary Questions
- **R**eason with Best Data
- **E**mergence

The pentagon may be flipped for delivery, to provide a framework for persuasive delivery, in the same way we flipped the Blue Pentagon for informative speaking. ("A Fire")

Persuasion Is a Process

It is known from the transactive model that persuasion is a process which occurs over a period of time rather than as a single event (Roskos-Ewoldsen 1997). Any information gleaned from a persuasive experience, including attitudinal shifts and behavior modifications, serves to become part of the input the next time the same topic is encountered (Nowak and Vallacher et al. 1998, 2020). The idea of persuasion as process would appear to give value to appeals of any length, as each encounter causes the listener to further strengthen or reject an idea. (Arpan, Rhodes, and Roskos-Ewoldsen 2013).

Emergence Theory has long been understood in the sciences, but has not been applied to human learning until recently. A chemist pouring one drop of a reagent at a time into a chemical solution may conclude that no reaction is taking place, because the solution appears to have remained unchanged. With the addition of a tenth drop, the solution suddenly bubbles and changes color. There is nothing significant about the tenth drop; the changes were occurring under the surface, yet invisible to the eye. The addition of the tenth drop was the catalyst which ignited the final change (Mighton 2008).

The idea that small changes take place without being visible may explain why one day a child seems confused by the rules of reading and the next day is able to read complete sentences. As emergence theory applies to human learning, it also applies to the understanding of new information in a persuasive message. While a short appeal may be insufficient to change minds completely, it is sufficient to plant a seed, which at a point in time, soon or later, will emerge to be the catalyst which changes minds.

Your job as a persuasive speaker is to **plant a seed.**

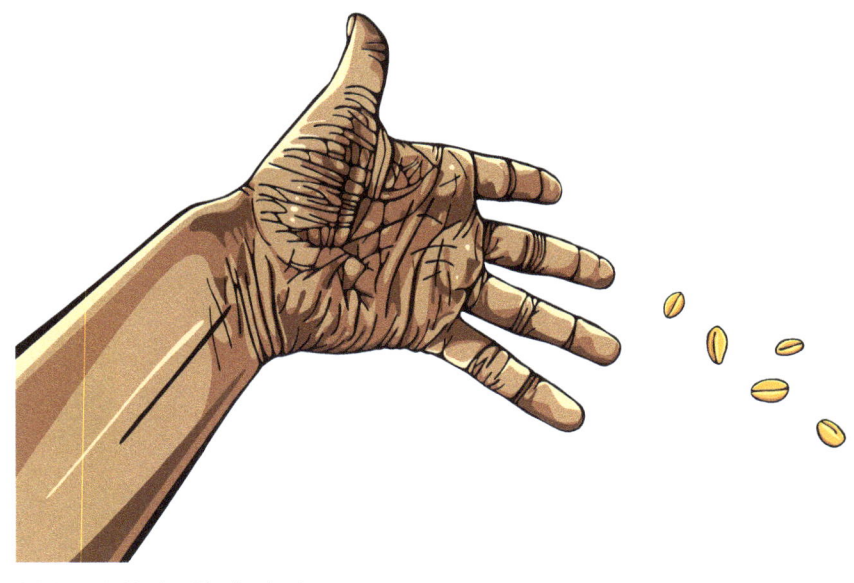

© Sylverarts Vectors/Shutterstock.com

Transfer the flipped **Fire Pentagon** to the **Persuasive Message Map**

```
                    ┌─────────────────────┐
                    │ Affective Experience │
                    └─────────────────────┘

        ┌──────────────────────────────────────────┐
        │       First Non-Leading Question         │
        └──────────────────────────────────────────┘
                            │
            ┌───────────────┼───────────────┐
     ┌──────────┐    ┌──────────┐    ┌──────────┐
     │ Boundary │    │ Boundary │    │ Boundary │
     │ Question │    │ Question │    │ Question │
     └──────────┘    └──────────┘    └──────────┘

      ( Data )        ( Data )        ( Data )

      ( Data )        ( Data )        ( Data )

      ( Data )        ( Data )        ( Data )


                  ┌───────────────┐
                  │ Emergent Seed │
                  └───────────────┘
```

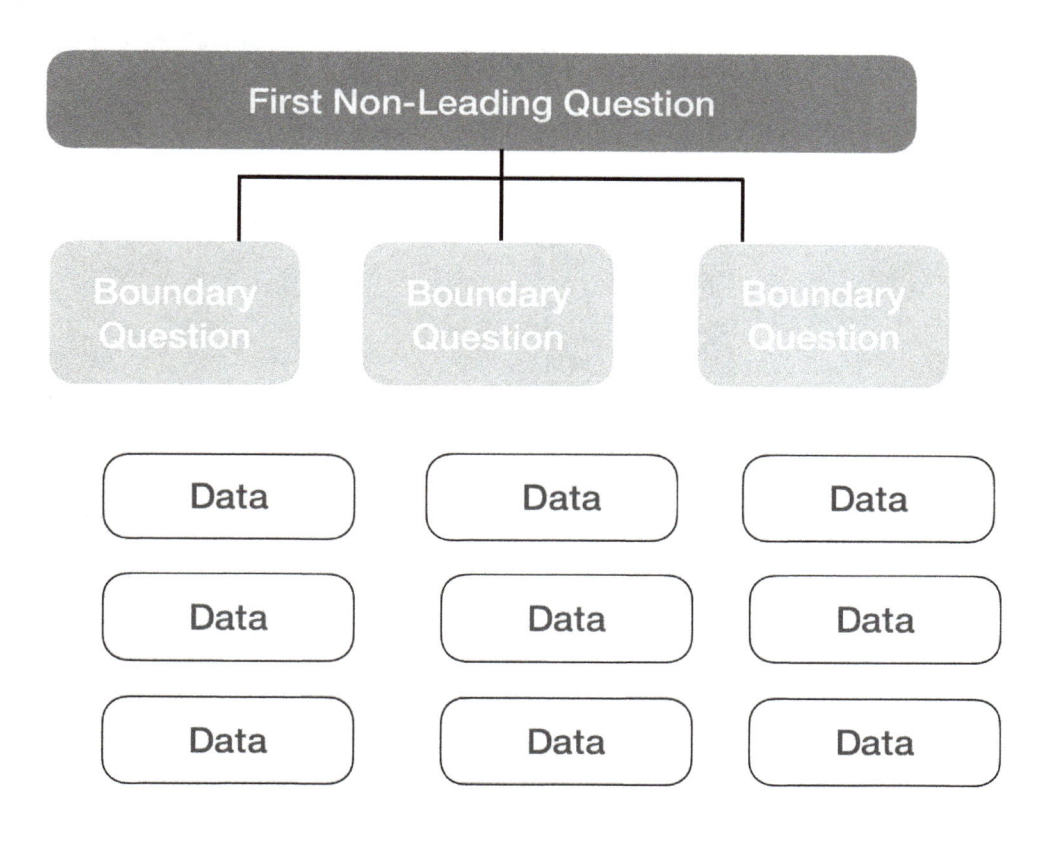

GAB LAB: The Playbook of Public Speaking Prowess Through Everyday Conversation

Take a moment to fill in the hand-out (Visceral Experience Exercise)

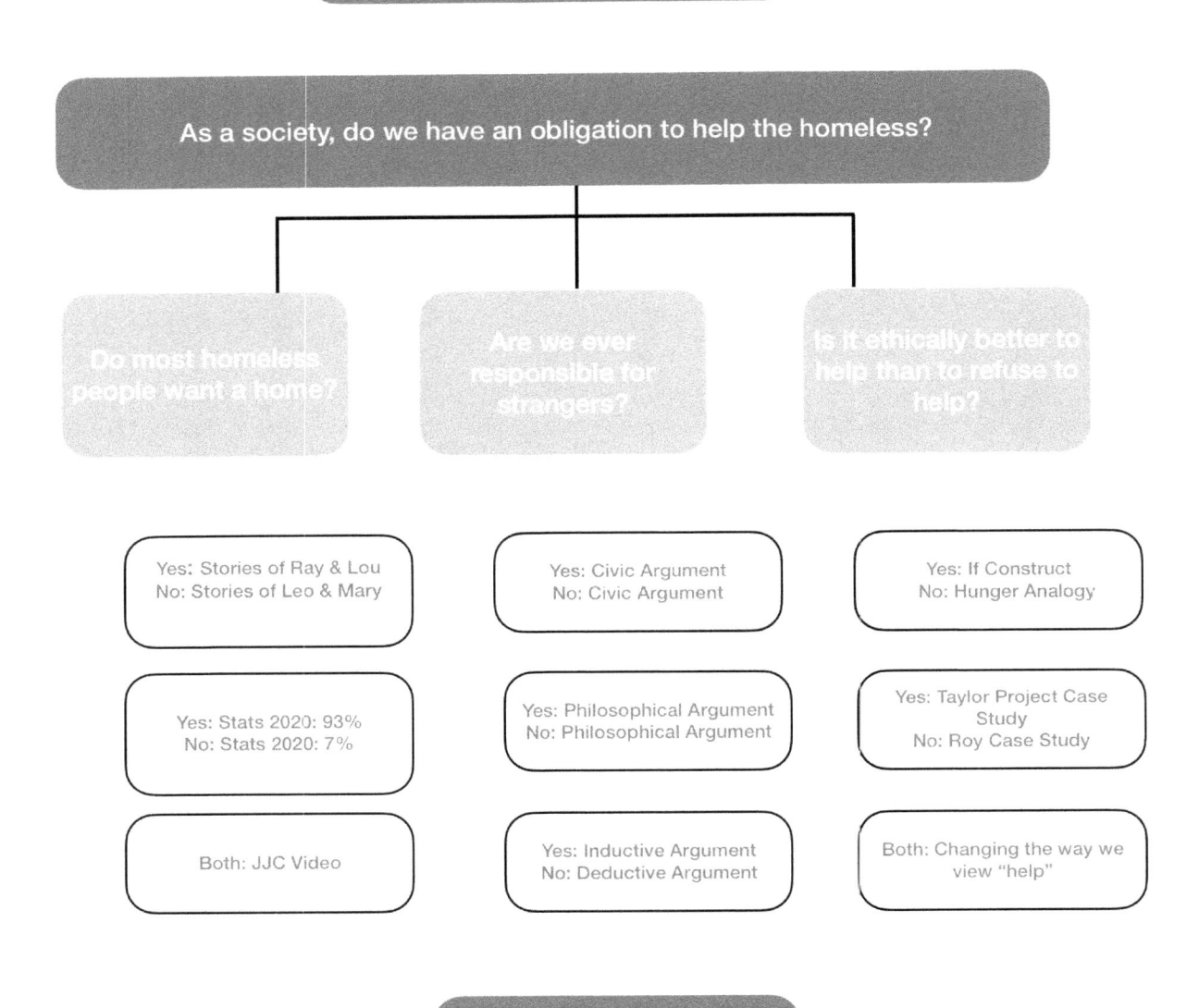

As a society, do we have an obligation to help the homeless?

- **Do most homeless people want a home?**
- **Are we ever responsible for strangers?**
- **Is it ethically better to help than to refuse to help?**

Yes: Stories of Ray & Lou No: Stories of Leo & Mary	Yes: Civic Argument No: Civic Argument	Yes: If Construct No: Hunger Analogy
Yes: Stats 2020: 93% No: Stats 2020: 7%	Yes: Philosophical Argument No: Philosophical Argument	Yes: Taylor Project Case Study No: Roy Case Study
Both: JJC Video	Yes: Inductive Argument No: Deductive Argument	Both: Changing the way we view "help"

Complete the new form. Compare. Remember the difference next time you have the choice to help.

Resistance

Even the best arguments may be met with resistance, as humans have been shown to be cognitively predisposed to resist attempts at persuasion. Fransen, Smit, and Verlegh (2015) identify four overarching categories of resistance: avoidance strategies, contesting strategies, biased processing strategies, and empowerment strategies.

Essentially, a listener may resist persuasive attempts by rejecting all data which contradicts his own viewpoint (avoidance) building counterarguments to contradictory data (contesting) processing emotionally rather than logically (biased) and finding or reviewing more data for his own position (empowerment).

If a persuasive appeal is designed correctly, every one of these resistance strategies may be eliminated or minimized.

Question-framed arguments prevent both avoidance and contesting; beginning a speech using soft data while minimizing and spacing the use of hard data prevents heuristic processing; engagement through exploration of data through boundary questions prevents empowerment.

Complexity of Persuasion

Persuasion is a complex topic.

There are many potential areas of discussion and numerous strategies for mastering persuasive argumentation. This chapter is not meant to be comprehensive, but a beginner's guide to excellence in persuasive speaking. A more detailed mastery-based approach may be found in *Street-Smart: A Speaker's Guide to Socratic Design.*

For now, here are three super-techniques for influence. These techniques are powerful, cognitive science--based, time-tested methods of making your ideas count.

Three Super-Techniques for Influence

Framing

Think of framing as the packaging of an idea.

Every time we share an idea, we package it. The package itself will affect how the idea is perceived. (Kahneman, 2011; Levin et al. 1998)

Imagine that you receive a gift from your friend Bob. He delivers a giant gold foil-wrapped box complete with a bow. Imagine how you feel as you lift the lid of the box. Now, you reach in and pull out..... a used dry erase marker. Be honest; are you excited or are you disappointed?

A little disappointed, right? The package raised your expectations, so that a used dry-erase marker seems like a real downer.

Now, imagine instead that one day, while you and Bob are working on a project together, you realize that you don't have a dry erase marker. Bob reaches into his backpack and pulls out one of his used dry erase markers (the same one, actually). He offers that you can use it and when you're finished he tells you that you can keep it. Wow, thanks Bob. That was nice, wasn't it? He didn't have to give you a marker at all. The marker is seen in a positive light. The difference in packaging and expectation affect how you view the marker—the very same marker.

The same principle applies to ideas. We package ideas by putting them into words. The specific words themselves make a difference. Think: pro-choice versus anti-life and pro-life versus anti-choice. The words affect our perception of the idea.

We can also frame ideas using various kinds of data. The percentage of people who die from overdoses every year will appear differently to us if we see a spreadsheet versus if we see pictures of individual people.

We can also frame by gain and loss. Positive framing looks like this: *Ninety-five percent of people have recovered from this disease.* Negative framing would be: *Five percent of people infected from the disease have passed away.* It depends completely on your intent. If you want your audience to focus on the negative, frame your ideas in the negative. If you want them to focus on the positive, frame the idea in the positive (Kahneman, 2011).

Make intentional choices about how you frame everything in a persuasive appeal. The packaging matters.

Analogy

Analogy is a comparison of two ideas based on their similarities. Perhaps you don't understand the role of breath in voice production, but if you are told that *breath is like the gas in the car and gives the voice its power*—it is easy for you to understand the role of breath.

Analogies are particularly useful in persuasive communication (Whaley and Babrow 1993; Sopory and Dillard 2002).

Analogies are particularly helpful when discussing controversial issues where confirmation bias might be problematic. When people are resistant to changing their position, they may stop listening to an opposition argument. We want to prevent or eliminate negative emotional reactions regarding topic-specific content. Analogies allow us to make a point *using a different topic* and then revert back to the original topic and reference the same point.

For example, if Bob struggles with obesity, he may not want to listen to another conversation about his weight. As soon as you approach the subject of diet, he may stop listening.

If, however, you approach the topic by asking Bob a simple question: *Bob, as my friend, If I were walking backward toward a steep cliff, but wasn't aware that I was doing it, would you tell me?*

Bob will say yes, if he is your friend. Then you confirm that you would do the same for him, because you care about him. Then bring the analogy back to the topic you *really* want to discuss. *Bob, I see obesity as coming close to stepping off a cliff. It's dangerous, and I care about you.*

When the desired point has been made, it smooths the path forward.

If Construction

When discussing hot-button issues, or issues which are highly controversial and may be met with additional resistance, the If construct allows the speaker to introduce potentially controversial information.

For example, instead of stating *Joe Jones was visited by an angel,* a controversial idea which will certainly be met with some skepticism, a speaker may state that *Joe Jones claims to have been visited by an angel* and point out that this is either true or untrue. Then the speaker will ask the audience to **consider the possibility** of the information being true. *I ask you to play along with me for a few minutes and consider this—what if it's true that Joe was visited by an angel? What does that mean for us here...?*

Generally people are more willing to consider an idea when it is not presented as being forced upon them, but when they are asked to engage, almost in a playful manner, to consider controversial data.

Ethical persuasion demands respect for individual autonomy. Only in true freedom can people make choices which effect significant and lasting impact on themselves and on the world.

EVERYDAY CONVERSATION PRACTICE:

1. Use a nonleading question any time that you wish to convince a listener of your position. Avoid stating your position explicitly. Lead your listener to discover the conclusion herself.

2. Use Socratic questioning to lead an opponent to your position by focusing solely on asking questions based on your opponent's responses. Avoid being confrontational. Play the curiosity card.

3. Respond to an argument with which you disagree by engaging the speaker using questions, rather than direct opposition arguments. Note how this changes the dynamic of the interaction.

GAB LAB: The Playbook of Public Speaking Prowess Through Everyday Conversation

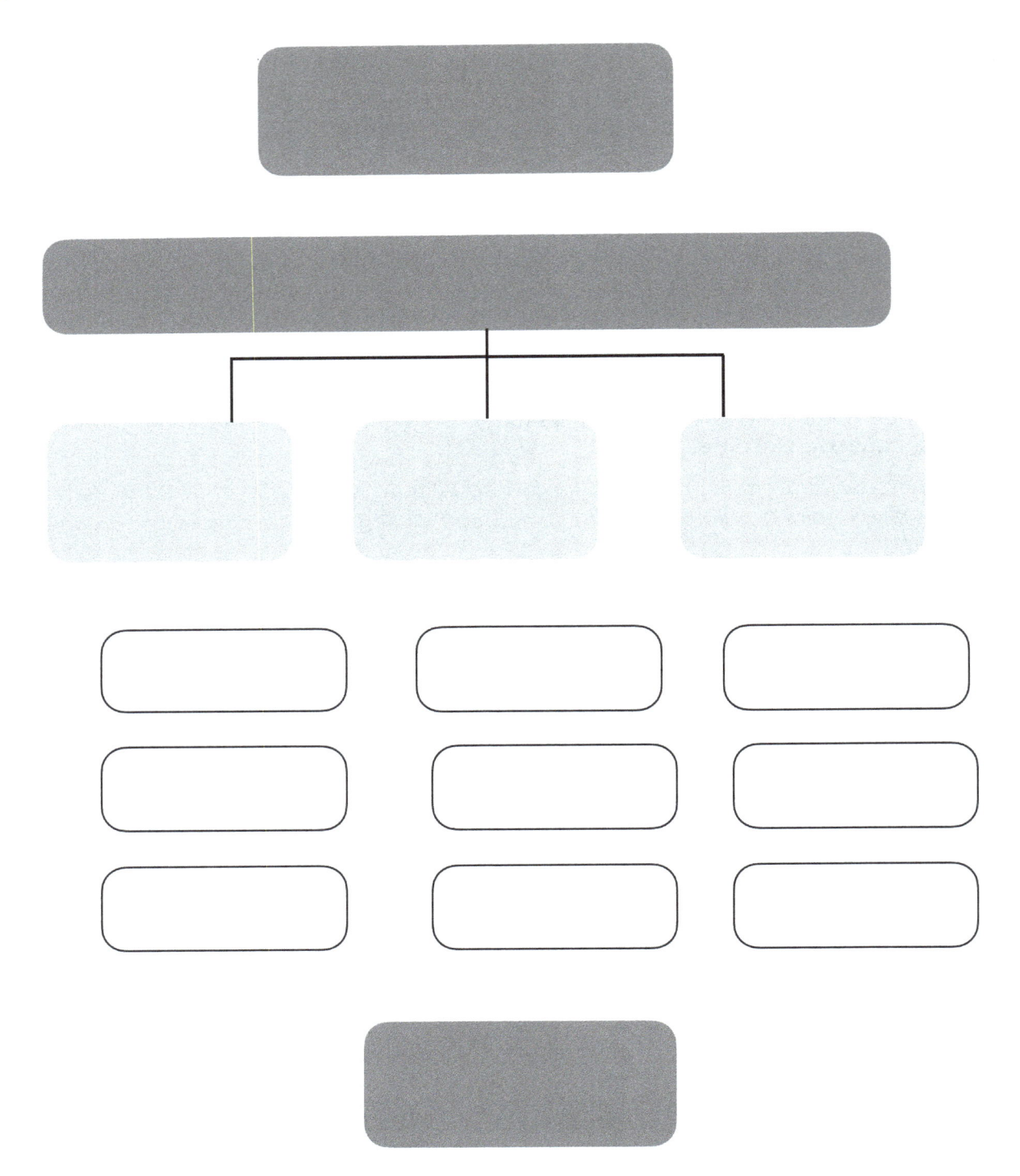

Celebrate
Special Occasion Speaking

© studiostoks/Shutterstock.com

Key Word: SPECIAL

Special Occasion speaking requires a greater degree of **formality** than other types of speaking. The act of recognizing a momentous event or accomplishment is in itself an **elevation** above the ordinary or mundane. It is fitting, therefore, that a speech delivered at such an occasion should be designed with care and attention and delivered in such a way that respects the solemnity or joy of the occasion.

While many special occasions are celebrated in banquet rooms and from stages, a smaller portion of them are celebrated in living rooms and on beaches. While the specific situation should be considered and respected, there is an argument for retaining the heightened nature of a formal address.

While we might refrain from wearing a ball gown to a beach wedding, we would still choose to dress well rather than showing up in ripped jean shorts and a crop top. A wedding is a special event and our choice to raise the bar on our everyday dress demonstrates a respect for the special nature of the occasion. In the same way, while a speech delivered on a beach may not necessarily begin with "good evening ladies and gentleman" the toast itself may be raised in a formal manner.

Protocol

There are specific requirements for each type of Special Occasion speech. These are the unspoken rules or expectations of special event speeches. It is a good idea to be aware of these expectations and to prepare accordingly. We want to avoid whispers of *"he forgot to thank the sponsor"* or *"why didn't he talk about Harry's illustrious career"* after having given a speech. Of note here: In this case, it is not so much worrying about what people think of us, but that we have been given a task which we have not properly fulfilled.

We will first discuss perspective and then give specific expectations or protocol for each type of special occasion address.

Perspective

In most cases, when being asked to speak at a special occasion, you are being asked to represent the group. It is crucial, therefore to adopt a manner of speaking which is inclusive rather than exclusive and which is representative rather than personal. This is one of the most common mistakes made by special occasion speakers.

Speaking on behalf of a group may be accomplished by:

1. Primary use of the pronoun "we" rather than the pronoun "I." This will allow the audience to feel as though you are speaking not on your own behalf, but on behalf of the larger group.

2. In the speech preparation process, you should gather information, stories, anecdotes from various people rather than relying solely on personal examples or stories. This will ensure that your listeners feel like participants rather than spectators.

Let's compare a toast to the bride given from both a personal (incorrect) perspective and a representative (correct) perspective.

Example:

Toast to the Bride (Incorrect):

*"Jane and **I** have known each other for ten years. Jane is **my** best friend. Jane and **I** used to attend the same schools and the **two of us** were college roommates. **I** have always loved Jane. Let **me** tell you a story about Jane and **I** when **we** were in college........ **I** hope Jane and Joe are happy....."*

Note: This excerpt above would be fine if it were a small portion of the whole speech, but it becomes problematic when the I/me perspective dominates the speech and when the speaker fails to include examples from other people, or other areas of Jane's life and to acknowledge that they are speaking on behalf of a group.

Toast to the Bride (Correct):

*"**On behalf** of **everyone** gathered here today, it is my pleasure to speak about Jane. Jane and I have been friends for ten years. **Many of you** have known Jane her whole life. Jane's **Aunt Mary** told me a story about when Jane was a little girl...**Roger**, a colleague of Jane's said that ... **We** all wish Jane and Joe the best......"*

In this second example, we can see that the speaker still mentions her own experience with Jane, but that she takes no precedence over anyone else in the room.

The following types of speeches require you to speak **on behalf of a group:**

Wedding Toast (unless you are the bride or groom)
Eulogy (Funeral Address)
Valedictory Address
Anniversary Toast
Introducing a Speaker
Thanking a Speaker
Presenting an Award
Master of Ceremony

You make speak solely on your **own behalf** for the following speech:

Thank You Speech/Acceptance Speech

Protocol

Greeting and Conclusion

Special Occasion speeches should include a formal greeting ("*Good afternoon ladies and gentlemen*" vs. "*Hey guys*"), as well as a formal conclusion ("*Please raise your glasses to toast Bob and Sally*" vs. "*Bottoms up everyone*"). This protocol is expected for all types of special occasion speeches and may be adapted according to the event. For example, "*Good Evening Colleagues,*" etc.

Specific Content

In order to deliver an authentic special occasion speech, you must be specific.

Don't be a living Hallmark card. "*You are special and brighten my day*" could (and does, that's why they sell them) apply to absolutely anyone. There is nothing personal about the card and therefore it can easily become less than meaningful. (Yes, the thought counts, but personalized thought would count more!)

Try to avoid cliches and platitudes. Because they are so familiar, we tend to hear cliches by not processing them at all; in other words, we don't think about what they mean. "*Jane is the love of my life; Lily's smile lights up a room; I knew from the first time I saw Joe, he was the one.*"

While these are lovely sentiments, and may be heartfelt, it would be much more effective to find a new and interesting way to express your feelings.

Use concrete examples to illustrate your ideas. Don't just say "*Bob is kind and generous.*" Give an example of Bob doing something kind or generous. The small details and specifics are what make a person unique. Failing to mention examples will make the speech unnecessarily abstract and may make it seem inauthentic. "*Bob is kind and generous and loyal. Bob is a hard worker.*" This one-size-fits-all kind of tribute is never memorable.

Humor

Humor may be used in any type of speech (including a eulogy) as long as it is used tastefully, keeping in mind that audiences often include people of all ages, from children to the elderly. Humor should never make people uncomfortable or embarrassed. Err on the side of caution. Not everyone has the same sense of humor and what is acceptable in your own circle, may not be the norm. Be mindful of feedback as you are delivering humor. If you have planned six racy jokes (not recommended) and the first two are received with polite laughter or people squirming in their chairs, avoid telling the last four jokes! This is an example of paying attention to your audience and adapting a speech accordingly.

Types of Special Occasion Speeches: Protocol

Toast (to honor a living person)

*Offer a formal greeting.

*Identify yourself and your relationship to the person of honor (unless this has been done already by someone introducing you).

*Honor the individual by describing their positive qualities.

*Honor the individual by mentioning their accomplishments.

*Honor the individual by explaining their contributions, etc., relevant to the context.

*Use a story or anecdotes to illustrate.

*Speak on behalf of the group, using examples from other individuals/sources.

*Be cautious with humor, especially at an event with guests of all ages.

© studiostoks/Shutterstock.com

*Avoid embarrassing the person being toasted. A toast is not a roast. Mention of ex-boyfriends, girlfriends, partners makes people uncomfortable. It's not the time or place for those references.

*Be mindful of the time. Don't make it too short (suggests lack of care or preparation, but don't make it too long, because, well that can be exhausting for everyone).

*End with a formal toast.

Eulogy (in honor of a deceased person)

*Offer a formal greeting.

*Identify yourself and your relationship to the person being honored (unless this has been done already by someone introducing you).

*Honor the individual by giving a chronology of their life.

*Honor the individual by detailing their positive qualities (without exaggeration).

*Be kind, but be truthful. Don't attribute qualities to people that they did not possess.

*Honor the individual by mentioning their accomplishments.

*Discuss the various areas of the individual's life.

*Use a story or anecdotes to illustrate.

*Speak on behalf of the group, using examples from other individuals/sources. This is particularly important in a eulogy as it may be the final tribute for an individual. If you are a work colleague of the deceased and you met him only five years ago, remember that he lived a long time before you knew him. Failing to include other perspectives disregards a significant portion of someone's life.

*It's ok to use humor, as long as it is done tastefully and appropriately. Use humor for the purpose of levity and people will appreciate the reprieve from the heaviness of the occasion. Turn the speech into a comedy sketch and you will be seen as being out of line.

*Try to end the eulogy on a positive note, mentioning the impact that this person has had on many people, or ending with a statement of hope if the individual held religious convictions.

Valedictory Address:

*Offer a formal greeting.

*Only introduce yourself if you have not been introduced.

*Reflect on the *past*.

*Comment on the *present*.

*Provide hope for the *future*.

*Speak on behalf of the group, from beginning to end. This is not your personal reflection on the past years but the group's collective experience. Include examples, anecdotes, stories from the whole group represented, including groups to which you do not belong. For example, if you were in the band but not on the football team, the band experience should not feature larger in the speech than anything else, as it is not representative of the whole group. Make everyone feel included.

© studiostoks/Shutterstock.com

*Avoid cliches and predictable themes. (It is easy to do with valedictory speeches. i.e. "life is a journey" etc.) Be unique and authentic.

*Thank those who have made graduation possible.

Anniversary Speech

*Follows the same structure as the graduation speech by addressing the past, present, and future.

Introducing a Speaker

*Offer a formal greeting.

*Introduce yourself (if you have not been introduced).

*Establish the speaker's credibility by outlining his or her experience, education, and accomplishments. (This requires prior research/communication with the speaker.)

*Introduce the speech topic and briefly preview a few main ideas.

*Do not deliver the speaker's entire speech! (Sometimes this material is made available to you prior to the speech.)

*Do not promise the speaker will give a great speech, or that he or she is a great speaker.

*You may instead express gratitude for the person's willingness to speak at the event.*Speak on behalf of the organization.

*Be certain that you are aware of the correct pronunciation of the speaker's name. Speak it distinctly and clearly.

Thanking a Speaker

*Be sincere. Look at the speaker, at least at the beginning of the address, without turning your back to the audience.

*Express your appreciation on behalf of the organizers, the audience, and any other contributors, such as sponsors.

*Mention a few highlights from the speech. Be sure that you don't plan these in advance as content may have changed since you last viewed the speaker's outline. Listen carefully to the content.

*Be brief.

Presenting an Award

*It is your responsibility to offer gratitude to a number of different parties: the organizers of the event, the sponsoring organization, the financial sponsors, the audience and other supporting parties. It is possible that there will be some overlap but it is possible that they will be discrete individuals or groups. Check carefully and be sure to thank those who deserve recognition. Often times the sponsors have a representative in the audience and if they are not properly acknowledged they may fail to offer the award in a subsequent year.

*Explain the history and significance of the award.

*Detail the accomplishments of the winner, specifically what distinguished them from other potentially worthy candidates.

*Present the award formally.

Master of Ceremony aka MC

*Being Master of Ceremony is a big job and is not for the faint of heart. An MC is the public face of an event. This job requires a lot of preparation and a good deal of impromptu skill.

*An MC is responsible for keeping the guests happy, keeping the event moving, keeping to a schedule, dealing with unexpected events, filling delays and delivering information.

*In order to be prepared for such duties, an MC should overprepare material for the event. Besides preparing the information to be delivered, you should prepare additional content which may be used to fill time and keep guests entertained. It is not uncommon for a served dinner to be delayed, for the band to be late, etc. The MC must entertain the guests so this time is not dead air and does not become uncomfortable for the guests. The MC should be a good model and not demonstrate impatience or frustration with delays.

*Prepare various kinds of jokes and stories and be prepared to deliver those which suit the particular audience.

*Here's a Captain Obvious comment: The audience should be able to hear and understand you. Unfortunately, many times it is difficult to hear an MC (or any speaker, for the matter). If you are the MC, you have the added responsibility of making sure the microphone is working, the speakers are not delivering feedback, the volume is adequate, etc. It is extremely frustrating when you can't hear the MC. Make sure it doesn't happen.

*Checking out the venue prior to the event is crucial, to avoid and prevent problems on the day.

*Be prepared for everything and anything. While it may not technically be your job to make sure the room is at a comfortable temperature, be sure that you will be the one who will have to deal with it. In advance, ask who to contact if certain problems arise. You will thank yourself for it later.

Thank You/Acceptance Speech

*This is the only time when it is acceptable and expected that you speak from your own perspective and not on behalf of an audience.

*Clearly, your job here is to say thank you to all who have made the award possible and who have helped you to achieve excellence. Think carefully about organizations, sponsors, supporters, competitors and the audience and be sure to thank all of them.

Celebrate 135

*It is a good idea to thank particular individuals, but if you are going to do so, be sure that you don't forget someone significant. It is a good idea to give a broad thank you as well as specific ones, just in case.

© SkyPics Studio/Shutterstock.com

*In addition to expressing gratitude, you should mention what the award means to you and what specific steps helped you to achieve excellence. The audience is interested in hearing a little more than thank you. After all, you have been singled out for recognition and the audience would like to see why and how you are distinguished.

*If you are presented with a gift, protocol says that you should open the gift in front of the audience. They don't want to witness you walking away with an unopened gift because it makes them wonder what you received. Open the gift graciously on stage. React with gratitude whether you like it or not. Avoid jokes which may be perceived as offensive. Opening a gift on stage might feel awkward, but it is an expectation.

*If you are awarded an envelope, however, do NOT open the envelope and comment on the amount of the cheque. This is considered to be in poor taste.

*Remember to acknowledge those who could have been chosen for the award. Practice humility, knowing that someone other than you is likely a deserving close candidate.

Remember that is an honor to have been asked to deliver a special occasion speech. You are representing a group and someone thought that you were deserving. Prepare, rehearse, enjoy and of course, **celebrate**.

© studiostoks/Shutterstock.com

EVERYDAY CONVERSATION PRACTICE:

1. Familiarize yourself with protocols; this will give you the confidence to speak up and be an impromptu spokesperson. On a small scale, even in ordinary situations we are called upon to thank an individual or a group of people, to express appreciation for a colleague or to speak a few kind words about the deceased.

2. Consider the degree of formality required for various types of everyday communication, such as addressing a superior, thanking a dinner host on behalf of a group of people, etc., and practice adapting your vocabulary to use the appropriate degree of formality.

3. Collect stories, jokes, and interesting facts to share in everyday conversations so that you will be able to garner audience reaction and see what works and what doesn't. If you are called upon to be a Master of Ceremony, you will have material with which you feel confident and may use if appropriate for the context.

Entertain

Advice to College Students
Dave Barry
https://youtu.be/HcQaAUUwdQo
© studiostoks/Shutterstock.com

Is Entertaining Itself a *Purpose*?

You bet.

There is inherent value in entertainment. We value relaxation and leisure time and we immensely enjoy being entertained. Just ask film producers, TV network executives and live music organizers. Entertainment is a billion dollar industry every year, in the United States alone (Watson 2020).

While networks used to see a decline in TV viewers during the commercial breaks, the industry quickly learned to keep audience attention by entertaining the audience *during* the commercials, while still promoting the product. This is an example of the importance of *primary* versus *secondary* purposes.

Every presentation, while containing various elements, always has a *primary* purpose. This primary purpose will determine the structure of the speech and will dictate the content. While informative or persuasive speeches may include elements of entertainment, they are not primarily speeches to entertain. Sometimes, however, the primary purpose itself is to entertain. While speeches to entertain may also inform, this should be secondary. If not, you are delivering an informative rather than an entertainment speech.

A commercial which entertains while trying to sell a product is employing two purposes, but its effectiveness will depend on its success at focusing the primary purpose over a secondary one. For example, a commercial may be very entertaining and the audience enjoys and recalls it, but if the audience doesn't remember what the product was, the commercial has failed in its primary purpose, which is to sell. Companies don't spend millions of dollars to entertain viewers. They spend millions of dollars to acquire new customers and sell new products, ideas or services.

You may be asked to deliver a talk to entertain guests at a golf banquet, to give a humorous reflection on ants at your son's Bug Hunter Club, or to offer some light words during the lunch break at a conference. While speaking to entertain is a less common purpose than speaking to inform or to persuade, it is certainly not an uncommon purpose.

Presentations, which are designed to entertain as a primary purpose, must have entertainment value.

What Is Entertainment Value?

Entertainment value, which is generally defined along the lines of "the quality of being enjoyable" is a rather vague and elusive concept. It tends to be subjective and audience dependent. We can, however, identify some universal qualities of entertainment value.

Qualities of Entertainment Value

*Gains and maintains audience attention

*Provides a pleasurable experience

*Engages the participant

*Fosters easy listening; does not require excessive mental strain

*Uses novelty and/or breaks expected patterns

*Provides an escape from the ordinary

Many of these concepts have been discussed at length in earlier chapters.

The same principles which apply to good speaking, in general, also apply to entertainment speaking.

In order to deliver entertainment value, we can use the Purple Pentagon. We will determine the answers to five questions in the preparation stage and will subsequently flip the pentagon and answer the five questions for delivery.

Preparation

What is the swag?

Everybody loves swag or free gifts. In the same way that we want to leave the audience with an action or plant a seed in other types of speeches, in a speech to entertain we want to leave the audience with something enjoyable to take away, like a *treat bag* at a party. We call this swag. Swag is something fun: a joke, a memorable idea, a great story, or sometimes even something physical like a logo-branded bouncy ball or a coupon.

How can I use showmanship?

Showmanship is your execution of the message. It is *delivery with punch*. Entertaining requires *energy* and lots of it. On top of energy though, think of how you can present yourself in an interesting way to the audience. Can you dress in a particular way which will add a little extra visual interest? Are you going to *sit* on a couch, a stool, *stand* on a platform? Do you want to be *funny*? Do you want to *inspire* the audience? Can you do *character voices*? How will you style your talk, as a stand-up comedy or a rousing inspirational rant? These choices will impact your delivery in very particular ways. The way you show up reflects your *personal brand*, or the way that people see you. Remember that small changes make big impact. This is the place to take risks and be bold; after all, you are an entertainer.

How can I actively engage the audience?

Entertainment is an experience. Make your audience active rather than passive participants. Be creative in finding ways to engage them. Can you get the audience to participate by actively *answering questions*? Can you have them participate in a *physical activity* or *move* around the room? Could they be given a *task*? Because we are social creatures, find a way to emphasize *social connections*.

For example, murder mystery parties are entertaining because guests have a mystery to solve (knowledge gap) as well as engaging with fellow participants (social connections) who are playing roles (transformative experience).

When you tell a great *story*, you engage the audience on a cognitive level as well as on an emotional level. When you use *humor*, you engage the audience by activating their pleasure centers, encouraging dopamine and endorphin production.

How can I transport the audience?

Because entertainment should take your audience out of the ordinary and into a transformative experience, it is your job to transport them. The earlier that you do this in your speech, the better. Think of your experience at a concert. Your experience doesn't begin when your favorite band begins to play. Your experience begins when you walk in the venue: the party atmosphere, the warm-up band music, the drinks, people laughing, the table with band t-shirts, etc. All of this forms a part of the totality of your experience.

As the entertainer, make choices which will help your audience to move out of the ordinary. Can you use *music* or *lighting* to set a mood? Could you have a *quiz, game,* or *interactive activity* to get participants talking to each other? How can you set up your *stage*? What about props? Think outside the box. How can you make them forget the world they came from and enter into your world?

What is the theme or through-line?

The theme or through-line is the *thread* between your ideas. It is important to have a cohesive structure even when you are entertaining. The audience should be aware of this connecting thread through your examples, your stories, your humor, your staging, etc. Sometimes you are given the theme; if you have been asked to give an after dinner speech to entertain guests at a hockey banquet, the theme is going to revolve around hockey. Other times, you are asked to speak to a group where the theme is not so obvious. Take your cues from the identity of the audience. Who are they? What are their interests? Dave Barry, the only comedian to have won a Pulitzer Prize gives a keynote address at the Competitive Enterprise Institute. His humor is based on private enterprise versus government jokes. He designs his subject matter for the specific audience.

For a general audience, you may choose your own theme. Keep the purpose of the event in mind. Certain subjects will be more appropriate for a pub crawl and others more appropriate for the office holiday party.

Think of how comedians structure their *humor*. Jokes are not chosen at random, but around common themes, as creative as they might be: *why my wife hates me on Thursdays; tips for international travel with a ferret; harmonizing with bald men; fishing with objects you already have in your car; etc.*

And on that note: **A Few Thoughts on Being Funny:**

Keynote
Dave Barry at Competitive Enterprise Institute
https://youtu.be/bTxSNuzQFxI
©durantelallera/Shutterstock.com

Use Specificity

What you will notice about the topics listed above is that they are very specific. *Specificity* is a strong choice because it allows for novelty, pattern interrupts and stickiness. Specificity facilitates humor. Note the difference between *"why my wife hates me"* and *"why my wife hates me <u>on Thursdays</u>."* Specificity adds an additional layer of ridiculousness and makes the whole idea a little funnier.

A lot of cars: Not funny

17.5 cars: Funnier.

I brushed against a tuna fish: Not funny

I brushed against the 4th rib of the skeleton of the tuna fish I had for lunch: A little funnier

Exaggerate

Things are generally funnier when they are exaggerated.

I had too many cookies yesterday: Not funny

Yesterday alone I had forty-two cookies: Smile-worthy

I won a small trophy: Not funny

I won a trophy about the size of an ant's left nostril: Funnier.

Found Humor

While it is certainly an option to tell canned jokes, it might not be your best option. Telling premade jokes requires a real sense of comic timing, not to mention getting the words just right. A little slip in the way you deliver the joke can make it fall flat. Most of us are not trained comedians, but that doesn't mean you should shy away from using humor. Having said that, don't force yourself to be funny if you're not comfortable in the space. Dead air after a joke is not the most encouraging way to build your speaking career.

Found humor is situational. Find funny things in everyday situations. If you find them yourself, you can be sure that your jokes won't be old and tired but fresh and real. Satire, sarcasm and dark comedy are a few styles of humor that you can use to communicate something funny. Making a social commentary by making fun of something is satire. Sarcasm is using a biting tone, in good fun and irony draws attention to the contradictions which are inherent in so many things. Self-deprecating humor is where you make fun of yourself. If you have enough confidence to do this, it can be a good way to be the *safe* brunt of a joke. What is not considered safe is to make an individual or group the brunt of the joke, unless you are absolutely certain that they are ok to play along with that. Sometimes celebrities are made to be the brunt of jokes because the audience will not usually take offence, but there is a risk in alienating audience members when you do this. You might not like a particular politician and make fun of him, while some of your guests think it is in poor taste.

Rule of Three

Professional comedians often suggest the rule of 3.

List three items/ideas in your sentence. The first two should be regular and expected while the third is the joke.

For example: *I went to the store and bought apples, pears and male Barbie dolls.*

This strategy uses the *pattern interrupt* concept because once the first two items are listed we notice a pattern. The pattern is "regular things that you buy at the grocery store." Therefore we quickly develop an *expectation* for the third item. We expect a third regular item. Since male Barbie dolls are unexpected, we find it funny.

There is a certain *comedic rhythm* with the use of three as well. It literally *sounds* funnier to say *I bought apples, pears and male Barbie dolls,* than to say *I bought apples and male Barbie dolls.*

A reminder for all humor: practice out loud. Because comic timing and rhythm matter in the delivery of a joke, it is essential to see how something sounds once you put it into words versus just trying it in your head, or worse, on paper alone.

Punch Lines

According to David Nihill, comedian and author of *Do You Talk Funny: 7 Comedy Habits to Become a Better (and Funnier) Public Speaker,* the order of your words matters. Put the punch line or punch "word" at the end of the sentence.

Let's say the punch line of your story is "and I found my keys on the table!"

Ask yourself, *what* is funny? That you found your *keys* on the table?

Or that you found your keys on the *table*?

If the funny part is the keys, put the word keys at the end of the sentence:

And on the table, were my *keys*!

Versus

If the humor is that you found them on the *table*:

And I found the keys on the *table!*

If you want to use humor, watch the masters. Note the choices they make and then find your own version of funny.

Purple Pentagon
Preparation
Flip For Delivery

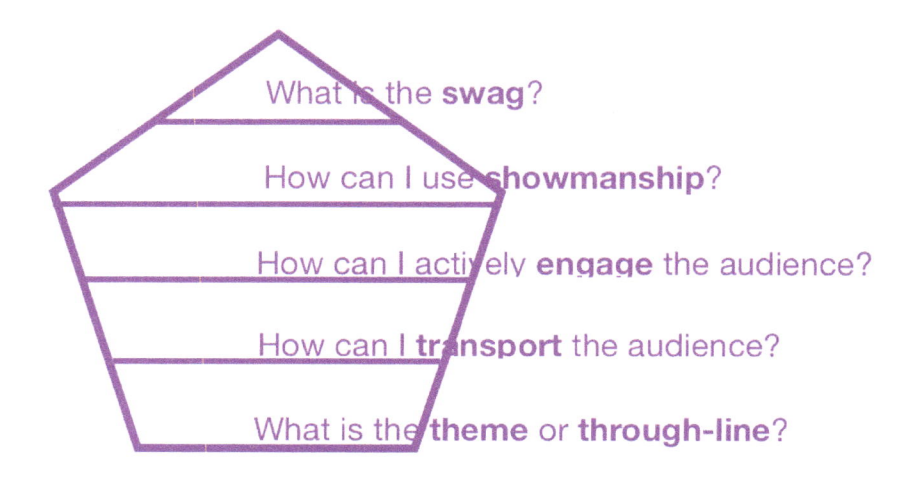

- What is the **swag**?
- How can I use **showmanship**?
- How can I actively **engage** the audience?
- How can I **transport** the audience?
- What is the **theme** or **through-line**?

- What is the **theme** or **through-line**?
- How can I **transport** the audience?
- How can I actively **engage** the audience?
- How can I use **showmanship**?
- What is the **swag**?

EVERYDAY CONVERSATION PRACTICE:
1. Start noticing humor in everyday situations. Get comfortable with throwing a little humor into a conversation or interaction.
2. Think about what kind of entertainer you are naturally. Start to notice how people respond to you. Do you get the best feedback when you tell stories? When you use imitation? When you try to inspire people? Work to finesse your existing strengths.
3. Step outside of your comfort zone. Not so comfortable with engaging an audience? Practice this at your next work meeting. Feel uncomfortable with the spotlight? Seek it out, even for a few minutes. Change is growth. Think outside the box. How do people expect you to act? We are living changing creatures and every day is a new day. Find your performance persona.
4. Memorizing and delivering poetry, scenes from plays or movies, or stories can be a great way to expand your performance skills. Tape yourself: audio or video or both. What do you like or dislike? Enhance your vocal skills, take an acting class, spread your wings. You don't need an audience to practice.

Public speaking prowess is in your hands, every day; it's as simple as having an everyday conversation.

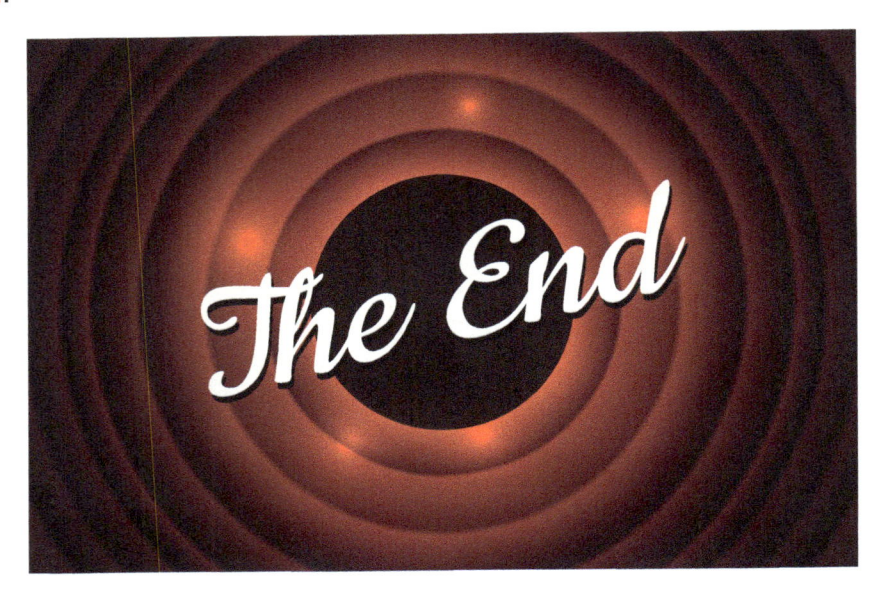

© Azat Valeev/Shutterstock.com

Citations

It's Just A Conversation

https://www.sciencedirect.com/science/journal/00225371

Levitin, Daniel. "The Organized Mind: Thinking Straight in the Age of . . ." Accessed May 30, 2020. https://www.amazon.com/Organized-Mind-Thinking-Straight-Information/dp/0147516315.

Paivio, A(1971) *Imagery and Verbal Processes* (Holt, Rinehart, and Winston, New York

Shepard, R N(1967) *J Verb Learn Verb Behav* **6**:156–163.

Stephens, Cheryl. Plain Language in Plain English. Vancouver, BC: Plain Language Wizardry, 2010.

Control Trumps Fear

Brown, Brene. The Power of Vulnerability. https://youtu.be/X4Qm9cGRub0

Campbell, Ali. "Chapter 7: Anchoring States." In *NLP Made Easy: How to Use Neuro-Linguistic Programming to Change Your Life.* Carlsbad, CA: Hay House, 2018.

Csikszentmihalyi, Mihaly. *Flow: The Psychology of Optimal Experience.* New York: Harper Row, 2009.

Jeffers, Susan J. *Feel the Fear and Do It Anyway.* London: Vermilion, 2019.

Zaharia, Catalin, Melita Reiner, and Peter Schütz. "Evidence-Based Neuro Linguistic Psychotherapy: A Meta-Analysis." Psychiatria Danubina 27, no. 4 (2015): 355–63. https://www.google.ca/amp/s/hbr.org/amp/2015/12/calming-your-brain-during-conflict

Impressions Matter

https://www.businessinsider.com/harvard-psychologist-amy-cuddy-how-people-judge-you-2016-1.

Mayer, Lyle Vernon. Fundamentals of Voice & Diction. Madison, WI: WC Brown & Benchmark, 1994.

McAfee, Kathy, and Leesa Wallace. "One Thought, One Person." In Sharpening Your Point. Indie Books International. 2019.

Attention Needs Attention

Arnsten, A., and B. Li. "Neurobiology of Executive Functions: Catecholamine Influences on Prefrontal Cortical Functions." *Biological Psychiatry*, 2004. doi:10.1016/j.bps.2004.08.019.

Hollerman, Jeffrey R., and Wolfram Schultz. "Dopamine Neurons Report an Error in the Temporal Prediction of Reward during Learning." *Nature Neuroscience* 1, no. 4 (1998): 304-09. doi:10.1038/1124.

Schultz, Wolfram, Wiliam R. Stauffer, and Armin Lak. "The Phasic Dopamine Signal Maturing: From Reward via Behavioural Activation to Formal Economic Utility." *Current Opinion in Neurobiology* 43 (2017): 139-48. doi:10.1016/j.conb.2017.03.013.

Data Overload is Dangerous

Chaiken, Shelly. "Heuristic versus Systematic Information Processing and the Use of Source versus Message Cues in Persuasion." *Journal of Personality and Social Psychology* 39, no. 5 (1980): 752–66. doi:10.1037//0022-3514.39.5.752.

Chaiken, Shelly, and Alice H. Eagly. "Communication Modality as a Determinant of Message Persuasiveness and Message Comprehensibility." *Journal of Personality and Social Psychology* 34, no. 4 (1976): 605–14. doi:10.1037//0022-3514.34.4.605.

Chandler, Paul, and John Sweller. "Cognitive Load Theory and the Format of Instruction." *Cognition and Instruction* 8, no. 4 (1991): 293–332. doi:10.1207/s1532690xci0804_2.

Heath, Chip, and Dan Heath. *Switch: How to Change Things When Change Is Hard.* United States: Random House, 2013.

James, W. What is an Emotion?. Mind, 19 (1884): 188–205. [Crossref], [Google Scholar]

Kahneman, Daniel. *Thinking, Fast and Slow*. London: Allen Lane, 2011.

Paas, F., T. van Gog, and J. Sweller. "Cognitive Load Theory: New Conceptualizations, Specifications, and Integrated Research Perspectives." *Educational Psychology Review* 22 (2010): 115–21. https://doi.org/10.1007/s10648-010-9133-8.

Petty, Richard E. "Creating Strong Attitudes: Two Routes to Persuasion." *PsycEXTRA Dataset*, 2017. doi:10.1037/e495742006-014.

Petty, Richard E., and John T. Cacioppo. "The Elaboration Likelihood Model of Persuasion." *Communication and Persuasion* (1986): 1–24. doi:10.1007/978-1-4612-4964-1_1.

Tversky, Amos, and Daniel Kahneman. "Judgment under Uncertainty: Heuristics and Biases."*Science*185,no.4157(1974):1124–131.doi:10.1017/cbo9780511809477.002.

Beware of the Competition

Bergen, Lori, Tom Grimes, and Deborah Potter. "How Attention Partitions Itself During Simultaneous Message Presentations." *Human Communication Research* 31, no. 3 (July 2005): 311–336. https://doi.org/10.1111/j.1468-2958.2005.tb00874.x.

Huff, Darrell, and Irving Geis. *How to Lie with Statistics.* New York: W.W. Norton &amp, Co., 2006.

Knaflic, Cole Nussbaumer. *Storytelling with Data: A Data Visualization Guide for Business Professionals.* Hoboken, NJ: Wiley, 2015.

Mayer, R. E., and R. B. Anderson."Animations Need Narrations: An Experimental Test of a dual-coding hypothesis." *Journal of Educational Psychology* 83, no. 4 (1991): 484–90. https://doi.org/10.1037/0022-0663.83.4.484.

Paivio, A. "Dual Coding Theory: Retrospect and Current Status." *Canadian Journal of Psychology/Revue canadienne de psychologie* 45, no. 3 (1991): 255–87. https://doi.org/10.1037/h0084295.

Roam, Dan. *The Back of the Napkin: Solving Problems and Selling Ideas with Pictures (Expanded Edition).* New York: Portfolio/Penguin, 2013.

Treisman, A., D. Kahneman, and J. Burkell. "Perceptual Objects and the Cost of Filtering." *Perception & Psychophysics* 33 (1983): 527–32 . https://doi.org/10.3758/BF03202934.

Tufte, Edward R. "The Nasa Story." In Beautiful Evidence. Cheshire, CT: Graphics Press, LLC, 2014.

Connect

Brafman, Ori, and Rom Brafman. *Click: the Magic of Instant Connections.* London, UK: Virgin, 2010.

Cabane, Olivia Fox. "Charisma Demystified." Essay. In *The Charisma Myth: How Anyone Can Master the Art and Science of Personal Magnetism,* 17–17. New York: Portfolio/Penguin, 2013.

Goman, Carol Kinsey. "Chapter 4." In *The Silent Language of Leaders: How Body Language Can Help-or Hurt-How You Lead.* San Francisco, CA,: Jossey-Bass, 2011.

Tal, Aner, and Aviva Musicus, and Brian Wansink. "Eyes in the Aisles: Why is Cap'n Crunch Looking Down at My Child?." Environment and Behavior 47, no. 7 (August 2015): 715–33. Available at SSRN: https://ssrn.com/abstract=2419182 or http://dx.doi.org/10.2139/ssrn.2419182.

Respond

Miss South Carolina Answers a Question. https://youtu.be/lj3iNxZ8Dww.

Beebe, Steven A., and Susan J. Beebe. "Patterns of Organization." In *Public Speaking Handbook.* New York, NY: Pearson, 2019.

Inform

https://www.ted.com/talks/bill_clinton_my_wish_rebuilding_rwanda?utm_campaign=tedspread&utm_medium=referral&utm_source=tedcomshare

Barkley, Elizabeth, and Major H. Claire. Student Engagement Techniques: a Handbook for College Faculty. United States: Jossey-Bass Inc., 2020, 102–08.S.1.

Chandler, Paul, and John Sweller. "Cognitive Load Theory and the Format of Instruction." Cognition and Instruction 8, no. 4 (1991): 293–332. doi:10.1207/s1532690xci0804_2. 1991.

Greene, A. J., C. Prepscius, and W. B. Levy. "Primacy and Recency in a Quantitative Model: Activity Is the Critical Distinction." University of Virginia, Department of Neurosurgery. Charlottesville, Virginia, 1999.

Heath, Chip, and Dan Heath. "Unexpected." In Made to Stick: Why Some Ideas Survive and Others Die. New York: Random House, 2010.

Schwarz, Eugene. "Prospect Awareness Scale." In Breakthrough Advertising, 29–40. Westport, CT: Titans Marketing, 2017.

Simon, Carmen. "Control What Your Audience Remembers." In Impossible to Ignore: Creating Memorable Content to Influence Decisions, 42–48. New York, NY: McGraw-Hill Education, 2016.

Stone, Vernon A. "Primacy Effect in Decision-Making by Jurors." Journal of Communication (1969). https://joc/article-abstract/19/3/239/4560914.

Paas, F., T. van Gog, and J. Sweller. "Cognitive Load Theory: New Conceptualizations, Specifications, and Integrated Research Perspectives." Educational Psychology Review 22, no. 2 (2010): 115–21. https://doi.org/10.1007/s10648-010-9133-8 2010.

Narrate

Brown M&Ms. https://youtu.be/_IxqdAgNJck.

Callahan, Shawn D. *Putting Stories to Work: Mastering Business Storytelling.* Melbourne, Australia, AU: Pepperberg Press, 2016.

Cin, S. Dal, M. P. Zanna, G. T. Fong, and B. Gibson. "Narrative Persuasion and Overcoming Resistance." *PsycEXTRA Dataset*, 2004. doi:10.1037/e633872013-232.

Leger & Association of Canadian Studies. April 2020. https://leger360.com/surveys/concerns-about-covid-19-april-28-2020/.

Oatley, Keith. "Chapter 3: Emotions and the Story Worlds of Fiction." In *Narrative Impact: Social and Cognitive Foundations*, edited by Melanie C. Green, Timothy C. Brock, and Jeffrey J. Strange, 39–41. New York: Psychology Press, Taylor and Francis Group, 2013.

Reinhart, Amber Marie, Heather M. Marshall, Thomas Hugh Feeley, and Frank Tutzauer. "The Persuasive Effects of Message Framing in Organ Donation: The Mediating

Role of Psychological Reactance." *Communication Monographs* 74, no. 2 (2007): 229–55. doi:10.1080/03637750701397098.

Schramm, J. D. *Seven Secrets for Storytelling Success.* https://youtu.be/jRmT-T7h16U.

Ted Blog: How to Tell A Great Story: Infographic

Yang Yang, Jill E. Hobbs. The Power of Stories: Narratives and Information Framing Effects in Science Communication. 2020. https://doi.org/10.1002/ajae.12078.

Zak, Paul J. "The Neuroeconomics of Trust." SSRN Electronic Journal (2005). doi:10.2139/ssrn.764944.

Persuade

Arpan, Laura, Nancy Rhodes, and David R. Roskos-Ewoldsen. "Chapter15: Attitude Accessibility: Theory, Methods and Future Directions." In Communication and Social Cognition: Theories and Methods, by David R. Roskos-Ewoldsen and Jennifer L. Monahan. New York: Routledge, Taylor & Francis Group, 2013.

Brehm, Sharon S., and Jack W. Brehm. "Persuasion and Attitude Change." Psychological Reactance (1981): 121–50. doi:10.1016/b978-0-12-129840-1.50010-7.

Brehm, Sharon S., and Jack W. Brehm. Psychological Reactance: A Theory of Freedom and Control. New York: Academic Press, 1981 [2013].

Cruz, M. "Explicit and Implicit Conclusions in Persuasive Messages." In Persuasion: Advances through Meta-analysis, edited by Mike Allen and Raymond W. Preiss, 217–30. Cresskill, NJ: Hampton, 1998.

Deci, Edward L., and Richard M. Ryan. "Optimizing Students' Motivation in the Era of Testing and Pressure: A Self-Determination Theory Perspective." Building Autonomous Learners (2016): 9–29. doi:10.1007/978-981-287-630-0_2.

Deci, Edward L., and Richard M. Ryan. "The Support of Autonomy and the Control of Behavior." Journal of Personality and Social Psychology 53, no. 6 (1987): 1024–037. doi:10.1037//0022-3514.53.6.1024.

Dillard, James Price, and Lijiang Shen. "On the Nature of Reactance and Its Role in Persuasive Health Communication." Communication Monographs 72, no. 2 (2005): 144–68. doi:10.1080/03637750500111815.

Dillard, James Price., and Michael Pfau. The Persuasion Handbook: Developments in Theory and Practice. Thousand Oaks, CA: Sage Publications, 2002.

Fransen, Marieke L., Edith G. Smit, and Peeter W. J. Verlegh. "Strategies and Motives for Resistance to Persuasion: An Integrative Framework." Frontiers in Psychology 6 (2015). doi:10.3389/fpsyg.2015.01201.

Heath, Chip, and Dan Heath. "Trip Over the Truth." In *Power of Moments: Why Certain Experiences Have Extraordinary Impact*, 97–101. New York: Corgi, 2019.

Hovland, Carl I., and Wallace Mandell. "An Experimental Comparison of Conclusion-drawing by the Communicator and by the Audience." The Journal of Abnormal and Social Psychology 47, no. 3 (1952): 581–88. doi:10.1037/h0059833.

Kahneman, Daniel. *Thinking, Fast and Slow*. London: Allen Lane, 2011.

Levin, Irwin P., Sandra L. Schneider, and Gary J. Gaeth. "All Frames Are Not Created Equal: A Typology and Critical Analysis of Framing Effects." Organizational Behavior and Human Decision Processes 76, no. 2 (1998): 149–88. doi:10.1006/obhd.1998.2804.

Mighton, John. "Chapter 2: The Emergent Mind." In *The End of Ignorance: Multiplying Our Human Potential*, 25–35. Toronto: Vintage Canada, 2008.

Nowak, A., Vallacher, R.R.: Dynamical social psychology, vol. 647. Guildford Press, New York. (1998)

Nowak, A., Vallacher, R. et al. Social Influence as Socially Distributed Information Processing. 2020.

O'keefe, Daniel J. "Standpoint Explicitness and Persuasive Effect: A Meta-Analytic Review of the Effects of Varying Conclusion Articulation in Persuasive Messages." Argumentation and Advocacy 34, no. 1 (1997): 1–12. doi:10.1080/00028533.1997.11978023.

Paul, Richard, and Linda Elder. "Critical Thinking: The Art of Socratic Questioning." Journal of Developmental Education (October 01, 2007. Accessed March 24, 2018. https://www.questia.com/library/journal/1P3-1447133181/critical-thinking-the-art-of-socratic-questioning.

Petty, Richard E., and John T. Cacioppo. "Effects of Forwarning of Persuasive Intent and Involvement on Cognitive Responses and Persuasion." Personality and Social Psychology Bulletin 5, no. 2 (1979): 173–76. doi:10.1177/014616727900500209.

Petty, Richard E., and John T. Cacioppo. "The Elaboration Likelihood Model of Persuasion." Communication and Persuasion (1986): 1–24. doi:10.1007/978-1-4612-4964-1_1.

Reich, J & Robertson,J. Reactance and Norm Appeal in Anti-Littering Messages: Journal of Applied Social Psychology. (Vol.9, Issue 1, 1979)

Rosenberg, Benjamin D., and Jason T. Siegel. "A 50-Year Review of Psychological Reactance Theory: Do Not Read This Article." Motivation Science (2017). doi:10.1037/mot0000091.

Roskos-Ewoldsen, David R. "Attitude Accessibility and Persuasion: Review and a Transactive Model." Annals of the International Communication Association 20, no. 1 (1997): 185–225. doi:10.1080/23808985.1997.11678942.

Sherif, M & Hovland, C. Social Judgment: Assimilation and contrast effects in communication and attitude change. Yale University Press. (1961)

Sherif, Carolyn W., Muzafer Sherif, and Roger E. Nebergall. Attitude and Attitude Change. Westport, CT: Greenwood Press, 1965 [1981].

Sopory, Pradeep, and James Price Dillard. "The Persuasive Effects of Metaphor: A Meta-Analysis." Human Communication Research 28, no. 3 (2002): 382–419. doi:10.1111/j.1468-2958.2002.tb00813.x.

Whaley, Bryan B., and Austin S. Babrow. "Analogy in Persuasion: Translator's Dictionary or Art?" Communication Studies 44, nos. 3–4 (1993): 239–53. doi:10.1080/10510979309368398.

Entertain

Barry, Dave. Advice to College Students. https://youtu.be/HcQaAUUwdQo.

Barry, Dave. Keynote: Competitive Enterprise Institute. https://youtu.be/bTxSNuzQFxI.

Merriam Webster. Definition: Entertainment Value. https://www.merriam-webster.com/dictionary/entertainment%20value.

Nihill, David. Do You Talk Funny? - 7 Comedy Habits to Become a Better (and Funnier) Public Speaker. Benbella Books, 2016.

Watson, Amy. Statista. 2019. https://www.statista.com/statistics/237749/value-of-the-global-entertainment-and-media-market/.

Printed in the USA
CPSIA information can be obtained
at www.ICGtesting.com
JSHW051214291123
52807JS00006B/22

9 781792 460388